365

activities

**you and your toddler
will love**

365

activities

you and your toddler will love

author
nancy wilson hall

consulting editors
dr. roni cohen leiderman & dr. wendy masi

illustrator
christine coirault

photographer
tosca radigonda

BONNIER BOOKS

GYMBOREE. PLaY & MUSiC

This edition published by
Bonnier Books, Appledram Barns, Birdham Road,
Chichester, West Sussex PO20 7EQ, UK

Gymboree Play & Music

Chief Executive Officer **Matthew McCauley**
Vice President, Gymboree Play & Music **Jill Johnston**
Merchandise Manager **Dawn Sagorski**
Senior Programme Developer **Helene Silver Freda**

Weldon Owen Inc.

Chief Executive Officer **John Owen**
Chief Operating Officer & President **Terry Newell**
Chief Financial Officer **Christine E. Munson**
Vice President & Publisher **Roger Shaw**
Vice President, Creative Director **Gaye Allen**
Vice President, International Sales **Stuart Laurence**

Managing Editor **Elizabeth Dougherty**
Editor **Karen Penzes**
Contributing Editor **Maria Behan**
Editorial Assistant **Lucie Parker**
UK Adaptation **Carey Scott**
Copy Editor **Jacqueline K. Aaron**
Proofreader **Gail Nelson-Bonebrake**
Indexer **Ken DellaPenta**

Art Director **Lisa Milestone**
Designers **Renée Myers, Britt Staebler**
Production Director **Chris Hemesath**
Photo Manager **Meghan Hildebrand**
Photographer's Assistant **Holly Brunkow**

a special note on safety

At Gymboree, we encourage parents to become active play partners with their children. As you enjoy these enriching activities with your toddler, please make safety your priority. While the risk of injury during any of these activities is low, please take every precaution to ensure that your child is safe at all times.

To reduce the risk of injury, please follow these guidelines: do not leave your child unattended, even for a brief moment, during any of the activities in this book; be particularly cautious when participating in the activities involving water because of the risk of drowning; ensure that your toddler does not place in his or her mouth any small objects (even those depicted in the photographs and illustrations), as some may pose a choking hazard and could be fatal if ingested; and make sure that writing and craft materials are non-toxic and have been approved for use by children under three years of age.

Throughout this book, we have suggested guidelines on the age appropriateness of each activity; however, it is up to you to assess the suitability of a particular activity for your child before attempting it. Ability, balance, and dexterity vary considerably from child to child, even among children of the same age.

While we have made every effort to ensure that the information is accurate and reliable, and that the activities are safe and workable when an adult is properly supervising, we disclaim all liability for any unintended, unforeseen, or improper application of the recommendations and suggestions featured in this book.

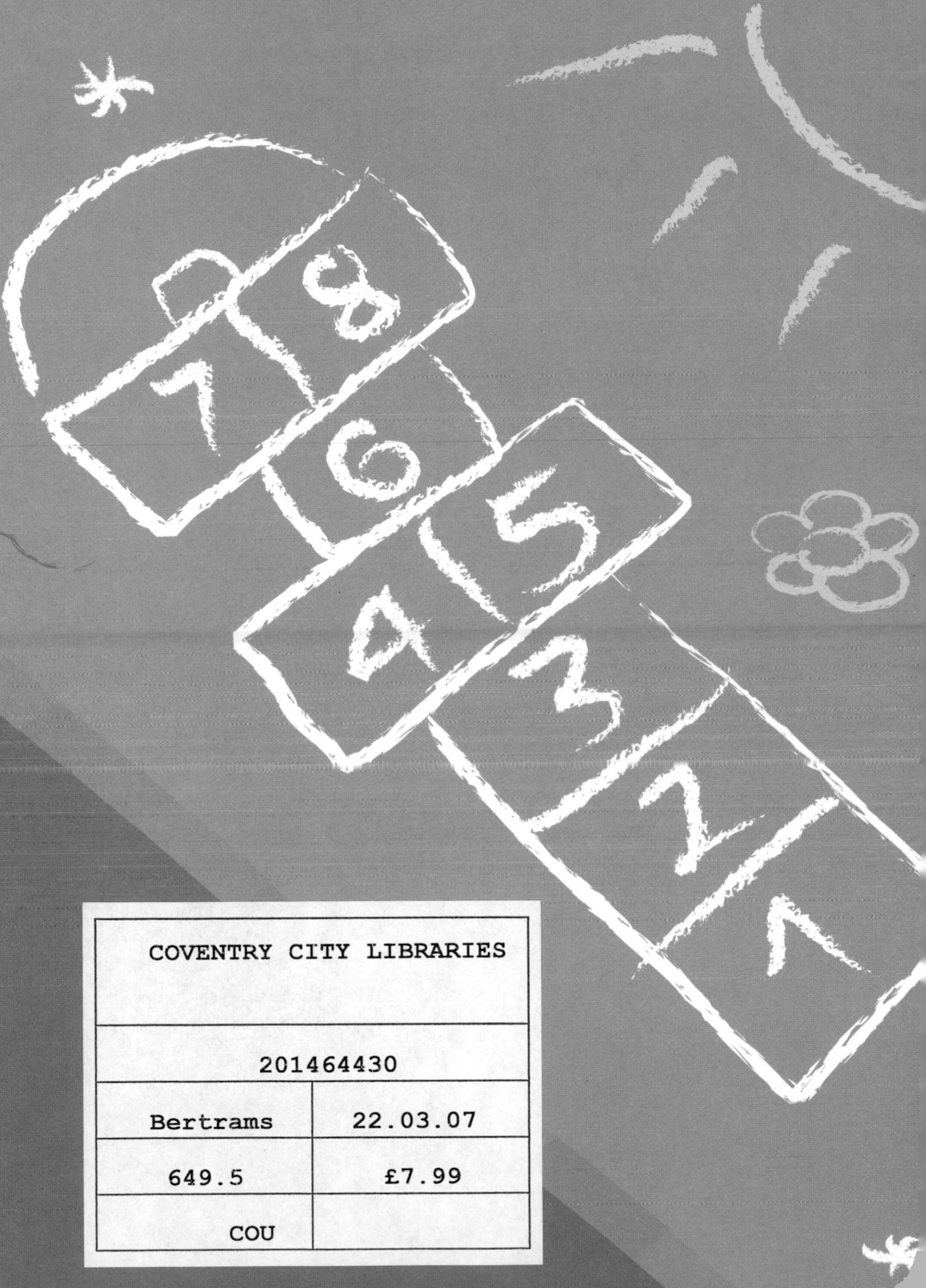

contents

24
months & up

181

30
months & up

273

Foreword

Welcome to the toddler years! Between the ages of one and three, children grow in amazing leaps and bounds. This is a magical time, as you and your little one laugh, talk, sing, discover, and find excitement in everyday moments. Playing with your child isn't just about fun and closeness, it's also one of the best ways to teach new skills, foster imagination, instil a desire to learn, and build self-esteem.

Many of the activities in Gymboree's *365 Activities You and Your Toddler Will Love* originated from Gymboree's popular Play & Music programmes.

That means they've been tested on thousands of children to ensure that they produce smiles, giggles — and learning. We are proud to offer this book as a road map for the journey through your child's wonderful toddler years.

Let your imagination take flight. Expand on our ideas, follow your child's lead, and create your own adventures together. As you nourish your toddler's mind and enjoy special times together, you are enhancing your child's potential and building a lifetime of precious memories.

Dr. Roni Cohen Leiderman

Dr. Wendy Masi

12+
from twelve months & up

Your child begins her second year as a great scientist, a fearless explorer, and an increasingly independent person. She loves achieving goals – even something as simple as opening and closing boxes – for the sheer joy of making things work. She's learning that there's a world out there beyond your lap, and she can't wait to experience everything in it. But it's your support, and her love for the people in her life, that give her the sense of security she needs to confidently take her first steps towards making the world her own.

1

mimic like monkeys

Little ones love to play "Monkey See, Monkey Do".
Take turns mirroring each other's simple actions such
as touching your nose and hiding your eyes, but keep
the game from going on too long by using a code
word to mark the end. How about "bananas"?

2

sing a counting song

"This Old Man" teaches counting, vocabulary, rhythm, and just plain silliness.

This old man, he played one,
He played knick knack on my thumb.
With a knick knack paddywhack, give a dog a bone,
This old man came rolling home.

In the next nine numbered verses, substitute the following phrases for "on my thumb":

Two...on my shoe
Three...on my knee
Four...on my door
Five...on my hive
Six...on my sticks
Seven...up to heaven
Eight...on my gate
Nine...on my spine
Ten...once again!

3

do a hat trick

A paper bag can become a hat in no time at all. Take
a medium-sized paper bag and help your child
decorate it with non-toxic crayons; leave the top 15 cm
(6 in) of the bag undecorated. When you're done,
roll the open end up the way you'd roll up a sleeve,
and presto – a funny toddler-sized hat!

4

pour it on

Offer your child a shallow tray of dry cereal and a
paper or plastic cup. Get him to watch as you fill the
cup with cereal then let him pour the cereal back into
the tray. It's a physics lesson and a snack all in one.

5

track the train

This simple fingerplay gets 'em laughing every time.

The little train goes up the track.
walk your fingers up one of your child's arms
from hand to shoulder

It says, "Choo, choo!"
tug gently at your child's earlobe

And then goes back.
walk your fingers back down your child's arm and
make sure the train takes a trip up the other arm, too

6

make a beautiful noise

Let your toddler rock out in the kitchen with pots, pans, and metal measuring spoons to clink together; plastic containers to thump on the floor; and some sealed boxes of cereal and dried pasta to shake.

7

push and pull

Sit on the floor with your little one, face-to-face with legs spread and the soles of her feet touching the insides of your legs so that a diamond shape is formed. Join hands and do a gentle back-and-forth stretch. Lean back slowly (but not too far), pulling her towards you, then change over, letting her pull you as she leans backward. Finish by leaning in towards each other and sharing a kiss.

8

do a tickly fingerplay

Make this quiet or noisy, to suit your child's mood.

Round and round the garden
gently circle one of your fingers around
your child's belly button...

Goes the teddy bear.
...make more gentle circles

One step, two steps,
slowly walk your fingers up his chest

Tickle under there!
softly tickle your child under his chin

9

reach out for fun

Attach a couple of favourite toys to your child's car
seat with short lengths of ribbon or plastic clips. That
way, they're at her fingertips for in-car play.

10

"comfort me...
Get me back on track when
I'm grumpy by pulling me into
your lap for a hug. Your support
helps me face the world – or at
least that jigsaw puzzle – again."

11

create page-turners

Make turning the pages of board books easier for little fingers. Punch holes at the top of each page, thread them with cotton, then tie the cotton ends and trim the excess. The cotton bumps separate pages so your child can easily find the delights hidden within.

12

inspire exploration

Explore a one-year-old's favourite concepts — open and shut, in and out — with supervised access to a variety of drawers, doors, and boxes. The better he gets at opening things, though, the more you'll need to lock up things that are dangerous or fragile. Consider devoting a drawer in the kitchen to your child, filling it with his toys and safe kitchenware to play with.

13

expand musical horizons

Add songs that aren't strictly kids' tunes to your child's
music library. Toddlers love lighthearted songs like
"Who Wears Short Shorts?" and "Octopus's Garden",
and will respond to most types of music. Mix what you
love – jazz, country, rock, or pop – with the little-kid
classics, and involve your child by dancing with her
and clapping out rhythms. Soon she'll have her own
favourites, and one day you may hear one on the radio
and she'll gleefully yelp, "They're playing my song!"

14

march like a mallard

Chant and march to work off kiddie energy on rainy days.

Little Ducky Duddle went swimming in a puddle,
A puddle, a puddle quite small.
He said, "It doesn't matter
How much I splish and splatter
I'm only a ducky after all!"

15

go crackers about art

Invite your child to "finger paint" on cream crackers with yogurt or pudding. When he's finished admiring it, he can eat his artwork.

16

pull my blanket

Place soft toys in the middle of a blanket or throw and let your child pull them around the room. Then let her ride while you pull (gently and slowly).

17

blow some berries

When you combine a "raspberry" with a kid's belly, you've created one of the greatest sensory experiences a toddler can have. With your little one standing in front of you or lying on his back, pull up his shirt to bare his tummy, gently hold his hands, and blow a raspberry right against his belly. He'll giggle when you do it lightly, but you might want to experiment with using a bit more gusto, too. The chances are excellent that the noisier you get, the more he'll laugh.

18

buzz a fingerplay

Here's one for your honey: sit facing
your child as you do this buzzy fingerplay.

Here is a beehive.
clasp your hands tightly together

Where are the bees?
hold your open hands out, palms up

Hidden away where nobody sees.
fold your arms across your chest

Soon they will come, flying out from the hive,
shade your eyes with your hand and peer out

One, two, three, four, five!
hold up your fists and open your fingers one by one

Buzzzzzzzzzzzzzz! Buzzzz!
with both of your hands up, flutter your fingers

19

play with laundry

Toddlers love to help. When you're sorting clean
washing, let your child pile socks or underwear into
a drawer or stack towels into a laundry basket. This
playful task gives him a chance to use his hands for
grasping and sorting, and it will make him feel like
a useful member of the household.

20

scope out the haircutters

Your toddler is more likely to take her first haircut in
her stride if she comes along on your hairdresser visits
now. Make it a positive event – sit her in the tall chair
and let her admire her reflection in the big mirror.

21

practise yoga

Get out some yoga mats or beach towels, take off
your shoes, put on soothing instrumental music,
grab a yoga book or DVD, and start stretching
together. Keep it fun, so the focus is on play more
than exercise. Don't worry about perfect technique
or holding poses for more than a few seconds.
Your child may enjoy yoga poses that mimic
animals, such as Downward-Facing Dog, Cobra,
or Cat. Finish with the Happy Baby pose — the
two of you can take turns *being* the baby!

22

drum some cereal

Have your child provide background "music" when you're hanging out together in the kitchen. Put some cereal in a large plastic sealable container, close it up, and let him shake away. For variety, give him wooden spoons to bang together or drum on the cereal shaker.

23

fly like a plane

Lie on your back and draw your knees towards your chest so your shins are parallel to the ground. Lift your little one up and lay her on her stomach on top of your legs, hold her hands, and gently fly her like an aeroplane. While making sure she feels secure, offer her a peaceful glide or a rollicking, dipping flying adventure.

24

"look what I did...
And I'm so proud!
I love your praise,
but sometimes
my mastery of the
world can be its
own reward."

25

share the social niceties

Understanding the social codes that help us get along with others will make your toddler feel like he's part of the adult world. So teach him to say "please" and "thank you" from the beginning, perhaps by playing games of handing objects back and forth. And most important, remember to say these words to him, too!

26

drop some clothespegs

Select a widemouthed container such as an empty cereal box and offer it to your child, along with some wooden clothespegs (the old-fashioned kind without springs). She'll have a great time putting the clothespegs in and taking them out. Before long, she'll be standing and dropping in the pegs from above, too.

27

march like ants

Get your toddler marching about the house as you sing and stomp this song together to the tune of "When Johnny Comes Marching Home Again".

The ants go marching one by one.
Hurrah! Hurrah!
The ants go marching one by one.
Hurrah! Hurrah!
The ants go marching one by one,
The little one stopped to beat the drum,
And they all go marching
Down to the ground,
To get out of the rain. Boom, boom, boom.
and continue, increasing the number and replacing "beat the drum" with

two...tie his shoe, three...climb a tree,
four...shut the door, five...take a dive, six...pick up
sticks, seven...pray to heaven, eight...shut the gate,
nine...jump out of line, ten...shout "THE END!"

28

bounce a knee ride

Try out this lively multi-character knee ride, increasing your bouncing tempo for faster and faster riders.

This is the way the farmer rides – walk, walk, walk.
This is the way the children ride – trot, trot, trot.
This is the way the lady rides – a-canter, a-canter.
This is the way the knight rides – a-gallop, a-gallop.
And whoa!
dip your little rider between your knees

29

start stacking

Now's the time for your child to begin experimenting with stacking bricks. Start with small stacks and react to collapses with a light "Uh-oh!" to avoid frustration.

30

take the nut people swimming

Fill a washing-up bowl with room-temperature water
(outdoors, you can use a paddling pool) and throw in
a dozen walnuts in their shells. Add a plastic cup and
a sieve or colander with a handle for scooping up the
walnuts. Give your child's budding imagination some
help — are those floating things the Walnut People?
Fish in the sea? Boats? One caution: walnuts will stain
some baths and sinks, so rather
than trying this in the bath, use
a pan you won't mind discolouring.
And always supervise water
play and empty the bowl
or pool when you're done.

31

join the club

Waving good-bye, which most toddlers have learned
to do by this age, both demonstrates and allows your
child to practise important motor and social skills.
Not only is waving good-bye a pretty impressive feat
of co-ordination, it's also like joining humanity's big
social club by knowing the secret handshake.

32

get some kitchen help

Give your toddler simple tasks to do while you're
in the kitchen together. He may enjoy putting wooden
spoons in a plastic jar or oranges in a basket. Even
if he isn't actually helping, he'll be practising
his eye-hand co-ordination and gaining a sense
of accomplishment as he completes each task.

33

learn about leaves

Collect leaves from your garden or a nearby park.
Look at them together, studying their shapes and
structures. In autumn, place dry leaves in a basket
or plastic container and let your child feel, smell,
and crunch them. In the spring, look for new leaves
just unfolding from their buds. Open up a bud to
show your child the "baby" leaf forming inside.

34

relax at mealtime

Want to keep mealtimes pleasant and avoid power struggles over food? Remember that a toddler can eat like a bird and still thrive. Don't make your child finish everything on her plate – she's learning to listen to her body and stop eating when she's had enough, which is healthier than finishing food she doesn't need. It's perfectly normal for your child to go through some periods when she doesn't consume more than a few bites, and some when she eats everything in sight. You might prepare an alternative if you're serving something she doesn't like, but it definitely isn't necessary – or a good idea – for you to become a short-order cook to make sure she eats enough.

35

make a merry melody

Chances are that by this age your child
has a few favourite songs that are staples in
his repertoire. Spend a morning singing
these favourites with him a few times then,
while you hum the melodies, encourage him
to sing the words. Or try leaving off the last
few lyrics so that he can finish the tune.

36

sleep under the stars

Place glow-in-the-dark star stickers on the ceiling above your toddler's bed. Make sure the lights have been on a while before bedtime so the stars absorb enough light to give off a comforting glow in the dark.

37

crown me!

Make a crown for toddler royalty by cutting slits in the middle of a paper plate – first two that cross the centre of the plate, then two more crossing these so that you create eight equally spaced points on the plate. Ask your child to colour the plate with non-toxic markers or crayons, then bend the points so they stand up around the rim. Now stage a lavish at-home coronation.

38

cook up a pancake special

Make faces in pancakes by using fruit or chocolate chips, and ask your child to name the nose, eyes, and mouth as you add them. Don't automatically offer sugar or jam — she may be perfectly happy without it.

39

sing a soggy song

This song is perfect for a rainy day.

It's raining, it's pouring,
The old man is snoring.
He went to bed and bumped his head
And couldn't get up in the morning.
Rain, rain, go away
Come again another day.
Little [your child's name] *wants to play!*

40

"enjoy my popularity...
But keep me from being
overwhelmed by friendly
strangers who want to play
with me before I'm ready."

41

get a sinking feeling

Fill a washing-up bowl (or a paddling pool, in good weather) and, making sure you're always supervising, bring out items for your child to experiment with. Does a cork float? What about a potato? Try lots of different toys and household objects, and sort them according to how they react in the water.

42

play "mirror, mirror"

Toddlers love mirrors. Ask your child, "Who's that boy in the mirror?" Watch how he reacts as you talk to him about his mirror image. Ask, "Where's the boy's nose?" If he touches his own nose instead of pointing to the mirror, he's starting to identify himself as a unique person.

43

take piggy beyond the market

Just about every toddler relishes playing "This Little Piggy". To get more mileage out of the game, try drawing out the last line: "And this little piggy – that's right, this one right here, no, not that one, not that one, but this very little piggy right here on the end, oh yes, this little piggy cried 'Whee, whee, whee', all the way home!"

44

start the day right

Routines give kids a soothing sense of continuity and predictability. A morning routine can gear your child up for the day ahead and, if it ends with one or both parents heading off to work, prepares her for the separation. So greet the day with a morning song, do exercises together, or go for a short walk to check the weather and pick up the milk from the doorstep.

45

tuck baby in bed

Help your child make a snuggly bed for a doll or a soft toy using a shoe box and some of his smaller baby blankets. When it's nap time or bedtime, help him tuck in the "baby" before he gets tucked in himself.

46

find the toy

Spread a tea towel on a tray. Draw your toddler's
attention to a small, brightly coloured toy. Play
with the toy together for a few minutes, then slowly
slip it under the towel while she's watching you.
Most one-year-olds will uncover the toy with a
flourish — she knows it is still there, even though
she can't see it. Once your child can do this
regularly, make the job of keeping an image of the
toy in her mind more challenging. Turn two plastic
cups upside down on the tray and slowly, within
her sight, hide the toy under one of the cups.
When she finds the toy consistently, she's well
on her way to understanding the concept of
object permanence (the idea that things and
people still exist even when they're out of sight.)

47

hit the hardware shop

What's better than a Saturday morning outing
to the hardware shop? The scent of freshly
cut timber, the dazzle of brilliantly coloured
paint samples, the feel of scratchy sandpaper.
To adults and toddlers alike, a hardware shop
offers up dozens of sensory possibilities.

48

hang out in a hammock

On a sunny day — even a chilly one if you're armed with a cosy blanket — it's great to snuggle up with your toddler in a hammock. To calm down, cuddle up and rock gently while you read a story together, talk, or just watch the branches swaying overhead.

49

make a shallow lake

Use a hose to make a puddle of water in a small plastic sheet spread over grass. Add plastic animals, boats, and dolls, and watch your child as she rules (and wades around and sits in) her watery kingdom. Always supervise her carefully — never leave her to rule alone.

50

get to know a ladybird

Look for ladybirds in the garden, or make your own by drawing black spots on cut-out circles of red paper and colouring in a black area for the head. If you do find some ladybirds, let your child hold one or two gently in his hand. Explain that they're good for gardens because they eat the little insects that eat our plants. They don't bite us, though they may pinch lightly with their tiny jaws. Let your child sniff one. Yuck! Ladybirds don't smell nice, but they're awfully good for our parks and gardens.

51

watch planes soar

Aeroplanes fascinate toddlers: after all, they're huge and they fly! Find a good viewing point (a park near an airport is ideal) and let your child study the planes as they pass overhead. Stretch her imagination by talking about where the planes might be going.

52

name body parts

Once your child can point to body parts like his ears, eyes, and legs, ask him to call out the names of those body parts as you touch them. Ask, "What's this?" then reinforce his reply by saying, "That's right. That's your nose." Then turn the tables and ask, "So where's my nose?"

53

"up and at 'em...
I love chances
to pull myself up.
And safe things,
like cushions,
to climb."

54

nurture baby dolls

Children often enjoy learning to nurture babies.
Toddlers especially love to take care of someone who's
younger than they are, an activity that helps them
develop empathy. Looking after baby dolls or soft toys
serves the same function — and they're fun to cuddle.

55

bag some toys

Hang a shoe bag — the kind designed to hang on
the back of a door — at your child's level. Invite her to
make a sorting game of putting away small soft toys in
the pockets. Line them up by type (for instance,
all the cats or bears), size, or colour.

56

mouse around

This song is a fun way to expose your child to the concepts of numbers and counting. Make up extra verses to rhyme with the strike number, such as, "The clock struck two...the mouse kissed you".

Hickory dickory dock,
clap your hands three times

The mouse ran up the clock.
run your fingers up your child's left arm

The clock struck one,
clap once over your child's head

The mouse ran down,
run your fingers down your child's right arm

Hickory dickory dock!
clap your hands three times

57

build a kiddie library

Books on shelves can be hard to get at, so a big
basket on the floor makes an excellent toddler
library. As your child's storybooks multiply, rotate
them so she doesn't get bored or overwhelmed
(but don't put away all of her favourite books at once).

58

test while you play

Play games that help you track your toddler's visual
development and hearing. Move toys back and forth
and in and out of his field of vision, watching his eyes
to see whether they follow the toy. To test hearing,
lower your voice and whisper something – make sure
he seems to hear and understand you. If your child's
responses seem off to you, discuss it with your doctor.

59

be a massage therapist

To give your child a calming massage, undress her down to her nappy and lie her on her tummy on a soft towel on the floor. Warm a dab of baby lotion between your hands, then stroke her back from shoulders to hips. Though all toddlers are different, many prefer a firm but gentle hand – not at all rough, but not too tickly and light. Move on to her arms and legs. Is she still awake? Repeat the process on her front.

60

hum a lullaby

Not every song has to have a fingerplay or a bouncing rhyme. A soft lullaby is perfect for times when your child is snuggled close to you, almost asleep.

61

throw things

Don't let toddler experiments with gravity – otherwise
known as throwing food from the highchair – get you
down. You might want to discourage that particular
activity by ignoring it, then rechannel his curiosity
by taking him outside to observe how different things
behave when he drops or tosses them. Biscuits, rocks,
feathers, and bubbles all move through the air a little
differently – and every bit of that data will be filed
away in your budding scientist's busy brain.

62

practise with cereal

Let your child practise her growing control of her hands and fingers. Put a small handful of dry cereal on a tray and demonstrate picking up the cereal pieces, one by one. Drop a few into a bowl, pour them out again, and let her have a go.

63

trot out a knee ride

Seat your toddler on your knees, facing you, and hold his hands as you "trot" your knees in time to this horsey rhyme:

Trot, little pony,
Trot to town.
Trot, little pony,
Don't fall dowwwnnn!

64

browse in a bookshop

Whether you pop in to check out the latest titles or come for storytime or a reading by a children's book author, bookshops offer lots of opportunities for fun and learning. Even if you don't manage to get out of there without some new storybooks, a bookshop visit is still inexpensive and valuable toddler entertainment.

65

sing dolly a lullaby

Nurture your child's tender side by singing to his doll.

Hush-a-bye, don't you cry,
Go to sleepy, little baby.
When you wake, you'll have cake,
And all the pretty little horses.
Blacks and bays, dapples and grays,
Coach and six white horses.
Hush-a-bye, don't you cry,
Go to sleepy, little baby.

66

do puzzles in pieces

The first time your child does a jigsaw puzzle, give
her just one piece to fit. As her spatial sense improves,
give her more pieces until she can do the whole puzzle.

67
get rolling

Get your child a low cart with a high handle – just right for him to grasp as he pushes it ahead of him. This kind of cart provides great stability for walking and, with a little imagination, almost unlimited play value. Today, it's a car; next week, a nest for a toy chicken and some plastic eggs; next month, a wheelbarrow for carrying sticks around the garden.

68
talk to the animals

Gather up some soft toys and arrange them in a circle around your child. Ask her to make each animal's special sound, then call on each one as if in a classroom: "Dog, you're next – a dog says...?"

69

have a rug toss

Throwing is easier than catching at first, and a small
beanbag animal or a rolled-up scarf can be easier
to handle than a ball. Bring out a few of them and a
small rug or a bath mat. Ask your child to stand close
to the rug and try throwing the animal or scarf onto it.
Then move the rug a bit further away to keep the task
challenging and help him build his gross motor skills.

70

chill out

Your toddler needs a little "me" time now and again.
So let her spend a few quiet minutes on a special
blanket on the floor to give her a quick break from her
busy day and let her practise amusing herself.

71

"let me get dirty...
Sometimes it's good to
be messy. But help me
tidy up afterward – clean
feels good, too!"

72

master advanced peekaboo

When your toddler is about a year old, she can understand that you'll still be there when you cover your face with your hands. She continues to love peekaboo, though, probably because she's old enough now to be in control and she may even initiate the game herself. Make it slightly more sophisticated by varying the way you play: peek around corners or over your newspaper.

73

carry some crayons

Time spent waiting for the doctor in the waiting room might feel long and nerve-racking for your toddler. But you can turn it into playtime with a box of crayons. Why do you think that lovely long sheet of paper is there on the table?

74

build a nest

Too cold or rainy for your little one to play outside?
Gather up all the cushions you can find and, since
you're the big bird, build a nest for her in a quiet
corner. Add a few soft toys (especially if you have toy
birds!) and a little cup of birdseed (cereal or small
crackers). Try this in the middle of the afternoon and
be ready with a soft blanket so you can tuck in
your little bird for a nap in her nest.

75

read the signals

If your child turns his face away, pushes his hands out at you, or puts his fist up by his ear, it might mean, "Just give me a moment here, OK?" But if he's raising his arms to you, grinning, or bouncing excitedly, he's raring to go and telling you, "Bring it on!"

76

perform a bedtime ritual

Develop a nightly ritual to help your child wind down for sleep. It might be a story and a cuddle, a few minutes spent talking in hushed voices about the best events of the day, or maybe playing a CD with a favourite song that will become her good-night melody.

77

do a wishy-washy fingerplay

Wash the dishes,
wipe your hand in a circular motion one way...

Wipe the dishes,
...and back the other way

Ring the bell for tea.
mime ringing a bell

Three good kisses,
kiss your child on each of his cheeks and on his nose

Three good wishes,
tap gently three times on his forehead

I will give to thee.
point to yourself and then to your child

78

nip biting in the bud

Teething pain, the lack of an appropriate verbal way
to express strong emotions, or even sheer exuberance
can lead your toddler to (literally) sink his teeth into the
world. Get to the bottom of his feelings, but make it clear
that biting isn't an acceptable outlet for these emotions.
If your child bites, gently take him to a quiet spot. When
he's calmer, explain that biting just isn't OK — ever.

79

hammer it out

Hammering is terrific fun for your toddler, and
it develops fine motor control and eye-hand
co-ordination. Look for toy tool sets or pounding toys
that she can use with your close supervision.

80

sing a song of fingers

"Where is Thumbkin, where is Thumbkin?"
raise your hands as if asking a question

"Here I am, here I am."
wiggle your left thumb, then wiggle your right thumb

"How are you today, sir?" "Very well, I thank you."
make your thumbs "bow" and "nod"

"Run away, run away."
hide both your hands behind your back, then
bring each finger out in turn and repeat with:

*Where is pointer? Where is middle finger?
Where is ring finger?* and *Where is pinkie?*

81

visit some animals

Make an excursion to a farm, a city farm, or a zoo, then
ask your toddler to name the animals he saw. Sing "Old
McDonald" and include the animals he met that day.

82

read together

Promote your child's love of reading by example. Have family reading times when everyone grabs a book and settles in. Your toddler can join a family member or look at a picture book on her own. Never leave home without a book to share with her in case you have to wait somewhere. In time, she'll come to see books and reading as one of life's great – and reliable – pleasures.

83

make a rainy-day sandbox

Put a plastic washing-up bowl on a tray and empty a box of oats into it. Give your toddler cups and spoons for pouring and digging, plastic horses for grazing, or toy cars and trucks for tunnelling through the oats.

84

follow the string trail

Kids love to explore, especially when there's treasure
at the end of the journey. Using brightly coloured
thread, wind a trail through your house. Supervising
carefully, help your child follow the trail as it runs
from his bedroom door, down the hall, loops around
the corner into the living room, then winds in and
out among the dining room chairs until he comes
to the thread's end, hidden in a box or bag that
contains a small treat. If he gathers up the thread
as he goes, the path will be easier to follow.

85

"encourage me...
It makes me feel great
when you let me know
about the new things
that I'm mastering."

86

choose some mood music

Pick different music to listen to according to your and your toddler's activities and moods. Be sure, though, that you enjoy times when the background noises are turned off and your child can hear herself think and listen to the natural sounds of her world. Give her the gift of learning to appreciate silence.

87

paint footprints

Unroll large sheets of paper on a washable surface (like the kitchen floor) and put a few colours of non-toxic liquid paint onto paper plates. Let your toddler step in the paint with bare feet. Hold his hands while he "paints" his footprints on the paper. Hang his creation in his room, or use it for wrapping paper.

88

try out new hairdos

Hang an unbreakable mirror on the wall behind the taps in the bath. To make washing more fun, use the bubbles from tear-free shampoo to sculpt hairdo shapes. Get creative with waves, cone-shaped spirals, and maybe even horns or a beard and moustache.

89

have a ball – or three

One ball is great, but a few of different sizes are even better. For kids who have mastered standing, kicking comes next. A soft rubber ball or beach ball about 25 cm (10 in) in diameter is perfect for kicking. Smaller balls are good for dropping and rolling, but be sure they're large enough so that they don't present a choking hazard.

90

free the feet

Until your child is walking on her own out
of doors, she doesn't need real shoes (nonslip
socks or booties will keep her tootsies warm).
When she goes barefoot in the grass, make
sure the area is free of sharp stones, sticks,
stinging insects, and litter. And check the sand
at the beach — it can be hot enough to burn on
a summer day. But as long as you're careful,
you and your toddler can enjoy the barefooted
pleasure of swishing through soft grass,
skipping along the water's edge at the beach,
or squishing through mud after a rainstorm.

18+

from eighteen months & up

The 18-month marker is a real milestone for your toddler. His expanding vocabulary makes real conversations possible and often leads to a riotous exploration of humour. His increased mobility sometimes has the reverse effect of making him clingy, as if he wants to reassure you that he's not ready to go too far on his newly agile legs. Increasingly nimble fingers help him build brick castles, throw balls, scribble, stroke the cat, and catch insects. He wants to try and do everything, but he still wants you close by while he does.

91

have high tea

Your toddler's growing imagination and improving language skills can lead her to create delightfully elaborate tea parties. Let her use a toy teapot to help you pour "tea" into the cups of her "guests", and serve biscuits or fruit. This isn't only pretend play – it's also great practice for future social occasions.

92

mind strangers

Your child will pick up on your behaviour with strangers, so teach by example. Keep him close when you're out and about so he can follow your lead about the people who make you feel comfortable and the ones who don't.

93

pack a travel bag

Stock a small rucksack with crayons, paper, a soft toy, a glove puppet, a book, a carton of juice, and a re-sealable container of cereal for your toddler.
This portable entertainment kit is great for tiresome journeys by car or train. Make sure she knows it's her rucksack — she may carry it herself!

94

pause for a poem

Your toddler will love the dramatic tension
if you both pause for a second after the
number "four" when you recite this poem.

The clock stands still
stand up straight and tall

While the hands move around.
move your arms around like the hands on a clock

One o'clock, two o'clock, three o'clock, four —
clap your hands with each number

Round and round, now touch the floor!
turn around on the spot and touch the floor

Cuckoo!

95

hit the beach

A beach is 360 degrees of pure surround sound —
and surround smells, sights, textures, and even tastes
(saltwater — what a surprise!). Protect your child with
frequent applications of sunscreen, a T-shirt, and a
floppy hat, then let him explore. Pouring, digging,
and piling sand; feeling the water on his feet while
you hold his hand; waving at gulls — all are great ways
to expand his sensory horizons.

96

issue a command

Now that your toddler knows more words and has a
better memory, following commands can become
a game. If processing one task is easy, challenge her
with more complex instructions, such as "Put the
book on the table and the teddy bear on the sofa."

97

get physical when you read

Reading to your child is about more than the words
you speak or the pictures he sees on the page. Help
him with language skills now and reading skills
later on by bouncing him gently to keep time with
the words, emphasizing the language's rhythm
by repeating words that sound good together, or
tapping out the syllables on your child's arm.

98

make an animal farm

When is a shoe box not a shoe box? When it's a barn!
Cover a box with red paper, cut out double barn
doors and windows, and place it on green paper.
Add a shed made from a cereal box, plastic farm
animals, and a sprinkling of shredded-wheat "hay"
for a complete farm experience.

99

play in the sand

For sandpit or sand-table play, give your child a variety
of cups, funnels, empty spice and jam jars with lids,
and colanders. Add water and supervise carefully as
you let her explore all of sand's tactile possibilities by
pouring, shaking, and shaping her "sandscape".

100

whip up some jellies

It's a snack! It's a toy! It's jellies!
4 packets unflavoured gelatin
2 cups cold fruit juice, such as apple or orange
2 cups hot fruit juice, heated until just boiling

The parent part: Pour the cold juice into a large heatproof bowl. Sprinkle the gelatin over the cold juice and let stand for 1 minute. Add the hot juice and stir gently but thoroughly until the gelatin dissolves. Pour into an ungreased 23-by-33-cm (9-by-13-in) baking tray and refrigerate until set.

The toddler or parent part: Use biscuit cutters (simple shapes work best for small hands) to cut out the jellies. Or just use a knife (definitely a grown-up job!) to cut the whole sheet into squares.

The toddler part: Poke the jellies with your finger. Stack them up and watch them wobble. Bounce them off your highchair tray. Oh, and eat them, too!

101

" today I coloured...
Let me talk about my adventures
at the end of each day. It helps
me exercise my memory — and it
also helps me to unwind. "

102

fill some big shoes

Challenge balance, encourage imitative play,
and have a laugh: let your toddler take a walk in
Mummy's or Daddy's shoes, literally.

103

lend an ear

Reinforce your child's growing awareness
of what his body is — and isn't! — with this song.

Do your ears hang low?
Do they wobble to and fro?
Can you tie 'em in a knot?
Can you tie 'em in a bow?
Can you throw 'em over your shoulder
Like a Continental soldier?
Do your ears...hang...low?

104

paint a "watercolour"

Let your toddler "paint" the outside of the house (or
the pavement, or the fence) with a bucket of water
and a big paintbrush. This is especially fun on a
hot day – and she can cool off by painting herself,
too – but always carefully supervise any water play.

105

get creative with cups

One of the best – and least expensive – toy purchases
you'll ever make is a set of stacking plastic cups.
Besides basic stacking, they're great for moulding
sand castles, washing a doll's hair, holding a "lake"
for tiny boats to float in, tracing circles, learning
about sizes...you name it. Just hand a set to your
toddler and watch what he does with them.

106

spin a spidery tune

For variation, try singing this popular song when your toddler is in the bath and encourage him to pour water out of a cup each time the rain comes down.

The incey-winsey spider climbed up the waterspout.
"walk" your fingers up in the air

Down came the rain
wiggle your fingers downward to make rain

And washed the spider out.
make a "wash out" gesture

Out came the sun and dried up all the rain.
form a circle with your hands above your head

*And the incey-winsey spider climbed up
the spout again!*

"walk" your fingers up again

107

do the wash

Toddlers love to imitate what you do, enjoy cleaning up, and are thrilled with water play. Combine all three by letting your child set up a toy laundry to wash his doll blankets, toy monkey's shirt, and puppy's ribbon collar. Give him a pan of warm water with just a tiny bit of soap, and another pan of plain water for rinsing. (Make sure you stay close by to supervise.) Improvise a clothesline, let him lie the items on a towel to dry, or help him pop them into the dryer.

108

lessen life's stings

Help your child cope with life's inevitable discomforts. When she takes a tumble, get down on the same level by sitting beside her or holding her in your lap. Acknowledge her pain ("That looks like it hurt!"), but don't fuss too long or too hard over minor accidents. With a scrape or cut, minimize the sight of blood by using a dark-coloured cloth to gently clean the area. When she's having an injection, get her to blow out as hard as she can as the needle is inserted. With a more serious medical event such as a painful ear infection or a cut that requires stitches, be her advocate and ask a doctor for the best way to relieve her pain. Studies have shown that healing is faster when pain is well controlled.

109

let your bookworm "read"

With your toddler's increased mobility and "busyness",
he may have trouble sitting still during storytime.
One solution is to hold him in your lap and ask him
to read to you. "What can you see here?" you can ask.
"That's right – a billy goat! What's the goat doing?
What do you think he'll do next?" Let him decide
when it's time to turn over the next page.

110

teach the bare necessities

18+

18 months & up

Though your little one enjoys trying to dress herself, taking clothes off is often much more fun than putting them on at this stage. Naked's great in the right context – so help her feel comfortable – but also explain that clothes are expected in most places. Going bare in the garden now and then can make up for having to keep her clothes on at the park!

111

hide and peek

While your child watches, hide two small toys in the room, and ask him to find them. Slowly increase the number of objects to keep the game challenging, but stop while he's still having success and fun.

112

sort it out together

Get your child thinking about how things are grouped into categories by getting her to help you sort clean washing. Have her find all the socks or all the shirts and place them in a basket for you to fold.

113

get a good feeling

Collect small pieces of cloth and paper of different textures: velvet, sandpaper, cellophane, wool, silk, tissue. Sit with your child and feel them together, one by one. "This one is smooth, isn't it? Does the sandpaper feel smooth, too? What about the furry one? It feels soft, doesn't it?" This stimulates his sense of touch and increases his vocabulary.

114

cook up a menu

Make a restaurant menu for home, with pictures of a few favourite healthy foods cut out from a magazine. Present it to your toddler at a mealtime, asking, "What will you have today, madam?" Being allowed to choose boosts her sense of independence, but the menu's limited options help avoid frustration.

115

play with food

Use a non-toxic marker to draw a trail of large dots on a piece of paper, and put out a bowl of crisps. See if your child can place one on each dot. As his fine motor control gets better, use smaller foods such as dry cereal pieces.

116

jingle bells

Securely stitch large bells to circles of waistband elastic that are big enough to slip onto your child's ankles and wrists. Join him in some dancing and clapping so they jingle and jangle. Make sure you are always around to supervise his play with these bells.

117

splash up a storm

Fill the kitchen sink with warm soapy water and throw in some plastic cups and bottles. While you're right beside her, let your child stand on a chair (with its back to the counter for greater stability) and play in the sink as long as you're willing to stand there (don't leave her unattended, though, not even for a moment).

118

"give me those gadgets...
Let me turn on your phone,
or stomp on the magic mat
that opens the shop door.
I love trying to work out
what might happen next.**"**

119

dabble with paint

Cut pieces of string into different lengths, up to about 25 cm (10 in), and dab them in pools of non-toxic liquid paint poured out on paper plates. Help your toddler drag the paint-covered strings across white or coloured paper to create abstract designs.

120

kit out your handyperson

Equip your child with versions of grown-up tools and equipment. Real but miniature garden tools, safe yet functional toy hammers and screwdrivers, and small brooms will help kids lend a hand around the house. And toddlers love to feel that they're making a contribution!

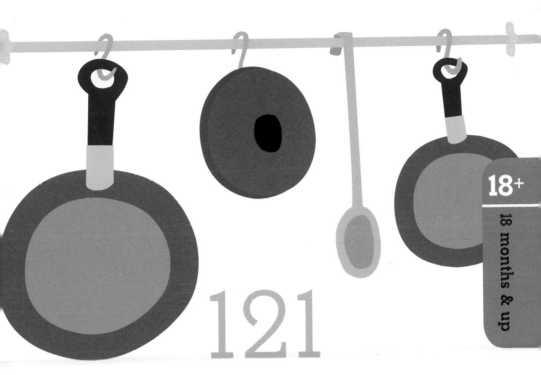

121

hail to the chef!

Your toddler is delighted when you ask him to
perform kitchen duty. He can put a clean towel away
in a drawer, carry his unbreakable cup to the sink,
or place rolls in a basket on the table. This is a great
time to get him used to the idea that everyone can find
a way to participate and help out. He's also probably
getting quite good at opening things, though, so be
certain to keep all materials that might cause injury
securely locked up or well out of reach.

122

blow some bubble art

Stir some non-toxic liquid paint into a little
bubble-blowing solution, and show your toddler
how to blow a storm of coloured bubbles onto
a large piece of paper. Voilà – instant soap art!

123

shake a tambourine

Two paper plates and a handful of dry cereal
make a terrific tambourine. Give your child some
crayons to decorate the bottoms of the plates. Then,
with the cereal on one plate, use non-toxic glue to
join the plates together, making sure the decorated
sides face out. Secure by punching holes around the
edge and lacing the plates together using a long
ribbon. Now put on some music and get shakin'.

124

bond with some bugs

18+

18 months & up

Lie face down on the grass with your
toddler and put any type of hoop or
a loop of string on the ground in front
of you. How many different creatures can
you see inside this little universe? Are
they eating? Working? Just hanging out?
Those activities sound like the sort of
things you and your toddler enjoy!

125

offer a choice

Toddlers prize their increasing independence, but they also need structure. If your child wants to choose her own clothes, narrow the choices: "Which will it be, the blue shirt or the white?" If she wants to pour milk on her cereal, give her some in a cup, not the whole carton. Let her make some decisions: "We need to go to the library and the post office. Which do you want to do first?"

126

stick on safety stickers

Putting themed large stickers on a sliding glass door at your child's eye level serves a dual purpose: it will help him see the glass door, and studying and talking about the stickers together will build his vocabulary.

127

hop on a bus

If you and your family go most places in the car, take a short trip with your toddler using a different mode of transportation. If you live in a city, ride a bus to a destination a few stops away or take the underground to the park. If you live in the country, you could take a bus into town or cross a river on a ferry. Supervise your child closely; hitting the road is fun but requires extra caution.

18+

18 months & up

128

create new sounds

Collect three plastic film canisters. Fill one with buttons, one with bells, and one with marshmallows. Tape the tops securely, then ask your child to shake each one. Watch him enjoy the sounds he creates.

129

blow a kazoo

If your toddler can hum, she can also make music with a kazoo. She won't just broaden her musical experience, she'll also produce some great sound effects: silly voices get sillier, race cars become vroomier, and ducks are quackier.

130

share smooches

Kisses aren't just a sweet way to show your little one that you love him. Kissing takes co-ordination and shows social and physical development. When your toddler returns a kiss, it means things are coming together for him: lip control, trust, taking turns, and the ability to express his feelings.

131

sing royalty to sleep

If you have a son, you can reverse these lyrics
so you're the queen and he's the king.

Lavender's blue, dilly dilly,
Lavender's green.
When I am king, dilly dilly,
You'll be my queen.

18+

18 months & up

132

make a bird snack

Encourage a love of animals by asking your
child to assist you when you go out to refill the
bird feeders and birdbath. To make a crunchy bird
snack, invite her to help you smear a pinecone
with peanut butter, then roll it in bird seed.

133

"**let me cling...**
Be patient with
me as I alternate
between being
a brave explorer
and your little
shadow."

134

make a library bag

Buy a plain sturdy canvas bag, and transform
it into your child's personal book bag. Use
non-toxic liquid paint to help her adorn it with
her handprints or with stamps made with apples
that have been cut in half and dipped in the
paint. Then use a fabric marker to add her name.

135

stack 'em high

Your child has probably graduated to stacking or
arranging about six to eight bricks by this stage.
Help build his architectural prowess – and his
understanding of size, shape, and balance – by
sitting down with him to build something a bit more
elaborate together, perhaps a castle or a skyscraper.

136

let your garden grow

Good garden help isn't so hard to find after all.
Young workers can pick up sticks, drop seeds into
holes in the soil, and water with a gentle
spray from a hose or a watering can.

137

create a land of cushions

Help your child build a place of her own out of all the sofa and chair cushions you can find. Stand them on end for walls, stack them for towers or thrones, and strew them around the floor for magic stepping stones. If the walls come tumbling down? No harm done – just stand them up again or build something new and even more fanciful.

18+

18 months & up

138

colour in the snow

Tint water with dark food colouring and help your child use it in well-rinsed squirt bottles to "draw" on the snow or to "clothe" a snowman. She can also decorate snow figures with ice "jewels" – coloured water that's been frozen in ice-cube trays.

139

greet another jack and jill

Is it a fingerplay — or a wingding?

Two little blackbirds sitting on a hill,
bounce your index fingers in front of you

One named Jack
wiggle one of your index fingers...

And one named Jill.
...and then your other index finger

Fly away, Jack.
turn one of your hands into a "wing" and flap
away, hiding your hand behind you

Fly away, Jill.
do the same with your other hand

Come back, Jack! Come back, Jill!
bring your "birds" back one at a time

140

explore a library's wonders

Your child can get a lot out of a trip to the library long before she's reading, so visit one regularly. You might ask about scheduled storytimes and activities for toddlers, or just go to have a look at the books. Most children's areas are noise-friendly and offer toys to play with and cosy reading spaces to curl up in. The concept of borrowing a book and giving it back the next week is hard to grasp at first, but soon she'll be eager for "library day" so she can change last week's treasures for new ones.

141

draw different strokes

By the middle of his second year, your child probably
can hold a crayon (the chunky kind is easier for little
hands to grasp) and even make deliberate strokes on
a piece of paper. Demonstrate drawing a horizontal
line, and ask him to try following your example. Then
do the same with a vertical line. If he's enjoying
imitating your drawing, move on to a cross. Then let
him scribble. (Bonus tip: if he decides to try out his
artistry on the walls, warming crayon marks with
a hair dryer makes them easier to wipe off.)

142

make a lantern

Have your child decorate a piece of paper with non-toxic markers. With her artwork on the outside, fold the paper in half crosswise, then cut 7.5-cm (3-in) slits at regular intervals along the creased edge. Unfold and curl lengthwise into a loose tube. Fasten edges with non-toxic glue, stand the tube up, and admire her fine paper lantern.

18+

18 months & up

143

avoid foul balls

Want a frustration-free ball game? Keep the ball from rolling off course by sitting across from your toddler with your legs open and his feet against the inside of your legs. Roll the ball back and forth inside the enclosed diamond shape that your legs form.

144

make a panda puppet

Fashion a panda puppet from a white paper bag, black paper, and a red non-toxic marker. Open the bag but don't unfold the bottom. Have your child put her hand inside with her fingers in the partly closed end of the bag, and you'll see where the face goes. Glue on two black paper shapes for eyes, two more for ears, another for the nose, a big black shape for the tummy, and two smaller ones for paws. Draw a mouth with the marker. Make several panda puppets and put on a puppet show together.

145

take a toy inventory

Make sure your child's toy box includes items that address a variety of developmental areas: bricks for fine motor skills; push-along toys for gross motor skills; materials for making or listening to music; lots of age-appropriate books; dolls and soft toys to encourage nurturing instincts; and playthings such as model cars, kitchen items, and dressing-up clothes to promote imitative and imaginative play.

146

welcome book choices

Encourage your child to look at books alone and to pick out ones you'll read together. You'll be surprised by how often his preferences change.

147

cook up some turtle pizzas

Take a ball of shop-bought or basic homemade bread dough — about the size of your fist — and pull off about a quarter of that piece. Form the first, larger piece into a flat circle — the turtle's shell — about 10 to 15 cm (4 to 6 in) across. Divide the smaller piece into six pieces. Use the small pieces to shape an oval turtle head, four legs, and a tail, and press them into their proper places on the dough. Spread tomato sauce on the turtle's shell, and have your child decorate it with grated cheese, salami slices, olives, or other toppings. Press two little olive bits into the turtle's head for eyes. Make a turtle pizza for everyone, letting family members choose their own toppings. Bake in a preheated 230°C (450°F) oven for 6 to 10 minutes, watching carefully to make sure your turtles don't burn.

148

18 months & up

"be my support...
I think I'm going
to be brave, but
then I get scared.
Thanks for not
laughing at me
or telling me off.
I'll be braver
next time!"

149

think inside the box

Toddlers this age love big boxes to play in, but don't expect complex imaginative play yet. Your child may not be ready to rocket to the moon in the box the television came in, but she'll relish the cosy space, the flaps to open and close, or maybe the chance to hide away for a nap with a blanket.

150

picture this

Put together a photo album of relatives and friends for your toddler. Look at it together and talk about the people you see: "Who's that? That's right, it's Aunt Kris – she's Molly's mummy." This type of album is especially good for kids with long-distance relatives.

151

recite a knee-bouncing rhyme

With your child on your lap and his hands in yours,
bounce this rhyme to teach the *feel* of language:

Intery, mintery, cattery corn,
Apple seed and apple thorn.
Wire, briar, limber lock,
Five geese in a flock.
Sit and sing by the spring,
O-U-T! And in again.
lower your child between your knees

152

print a rainbow

Draw an outline of a rainbow. Mix small amounts
of non-toxic liquid paint, and have your child fill
the rainbow with her colourful fingerprints.

153

walk and talk

As you're walking with your child around your neighbourhood, tease his imagination and get him thinking about the people in his surroundings. Stop outside a house and talk to him about what might be going on inside: "I see a pushchair. Do you think a baby lives there? And there's a lead on the porch — they must have a puppy!"

154

make a "quiet kit"

Place an activity basket near the phone to buy a few minutes of quiet when you have to make or take an important call. Include toys that aren't noisy, a small torch, and some glove puppets that only whisper.

155

dig some dinosaurs

Why do tiny people love enormous animals? Maybe because in their budding imaginations they're starting to see themselves as larger, more powerful creatures. Your child may love dinosaur toys, and as he gets older — and better at longer outings — he might enjoy dinosaur events at museums, too.

156

do some target practice

Roll down the top edges of three paper
bags to make a short, a medium, and a tall basket
for throwing practice. Give your child some
soft objects like sponges, and ask him to aim
at the shortest and closest basket first, then
move on to the taller targets further away.

157

play some name games

Towards the middle of your child's second year, start
pointing out her name in print. Emphasize her first
initial and talk about other words that share the
same initial sound. "Dog starts the same way
your name does – listen: d-d-d-dog, D-D-D-Dana!"

158

save the bunny

This fingerplay appeals to kids' nurturing instincts.

In a cabin in the woods,
a small child by the window stood,
touch your fingers together to make a roof over your
head; use your index finger to draw a square window

Saw a rabbit hopping near, knocking at the door.
making a peace sign for the rabbit's ears,
"hop" your hand in front of you

"Help me, help me" – the rabbit cried,
"I just need a place to hide."
throw your arms up twice in alarm

"Come little rabbit, come inside,
wave your hand towards you to beckon the rabbit

I'll take care of you."

159

row that boat

Exercise your child's motor skills and balance
by having him "row" with a plush toy seated in his lap.

Row, row, row your boat
Gently down the stream.
Merrily, merrily, merrily, merrily,
Life is but a dream.

160

feel with feet

Broaden your toddler's sensory knowledge by giving
her a few large plastic tubs of squidgy, sandy, and
gooey substances like mud, sand, and jelly. Watch her
plunge in and explore the world anew — with her feet.

161

separate gently

The parenting books said your toddler would
go through separation anxiety at nine months,
and the chances are she did. But she'll still have
days when she's clingy, so respect her feelings and
allow extra transition time when you need to leave.

162

play ring around the rosy

Gather a gang of kids and show them how to
join hands in a circle and collapse at the appropriate
time. Or grasp both your child's hands and dance
around in a small circle just for two.

Ring around the rosy, pocket full of posies.
Attishoo, attishoo, we all fall DOWN!

163

"let's play hide and seek...
I can explore what it feels
like to be away from you
as well as how great it feels
to be found."

164

pat that cake

This active version of "Patty Cake" is perfect
for your toddler's fine motor skill practice.

18+

18 months & up

Patty cake, patty cake,
Baker's man,
Bake me a cake
As fast as you can.
clap your hands against his for the first few lines

Pat it,
both of you mime stirring a big bowl of dough

And prick it,
pretend to be rolling out the dough together

And mark it with a B,
use your index finger to trace the letter
in the air or on his tummy

And put it in the oven
both of you mime sliding the cake in the oven

For Baby and me!
gently poke his tummy, then your own

165

enjoy nature in the city

Can't make it to the countryside this weekend?
A trip to a garden centre is free entertainment,
though it may be hard to resist bringing home
some little green friends. Supervise closely as your
toddler wanders through a forest of plants. When
you're only a few feet tall, a leafy, misty greenhouse
becomes an Amazon rainforest, a tray of cactus is a
desert landscape, and the display of fountains and
birdbaths looks like a pint-sized lake district.

166

zip, snap, button!

At 18 months, your toddler is developing the fine
motor control and self-care skills to help dress
himself. Find a book or a doll that lets him practise
with buttons, zips, and other fasteners. Clothes that
have roomy necks, big buttons, and zips with large
pull tabs help at this "I did it myself!" stage.

167

strum a tune

Make a nifty string instrument by wrapping several
rubber bands lengthwise around a box with an open
top or a hole in the top. A sturdy shoe box or a tissue
box works well. Supervise your child closely as she
strums in case one of her "strings" comes loose.

168

check out the playground

A playground boasts more play equipment than you have room for in your garden, and often has a child-safe material underfoot to make falls less hazardous. For a child this age attractions such as hiding places to look out of, low surfaces and inclines to climb over, and sandpits to dig in are great.

169

give kitty a thrill

Dim the lights and let your toddler provide a torch "mouse" for a cat to chase. This is a great way for a young child who might be a little nervous about touching a cat to interact with him. Besides, playing with a torch is always fun!

170

play favourites

There are times when only Mummy will do. Or only Daddy. Or only the babysitter. Don't be offended if your child plays favourites. She's getting to know the people in her life and learning to appreciate their different styles. It won't take her long to work out that Grandad swings her just right, or that Aunt Maria does the best monkey imitation.

171

jazz up a shirt

Keep the root end from a bunch of celery and help your child use it as a stamp to decorate a T-shirt. Dab the celery "stamp" in non-toxic paint and, with a sheet of cardboard inside the shirt to keep the design from bleeding through, stamp away. Once the shirt's dry, run it through a warm dryer for 20 minutes to make the design last longer.

172

make edible art

Finger paint with instant pudding. Strip your little one down to her nappy and give her some big sheets of paper and a plastic bowl of pudding so she can make some sweet artwork.

173

let those feelings out

Sometimes a day away from you may end with a flare-up. Even if your toddler had a great time, he may be tired and ready to release the strong feelings that built up during the day. And who better to share those feelings with than you, the person he feels safest with? So if he needs to let off a little steam, let him.

174

reassure your trooper

Your child's fears can be fickle: one day the neighbour's dog and the giant model of the lobster are funny; the next, they're downright creepy. Don't make a big deal out of these fears. Let your child know that she's safe – and that you're there to look out for her.

175

do some milky magic

Pour a cup of milk into a shallow round bowl. Get your child to watch as you carefully – without stirring – drop four drops of food colouring randomly onto the surface of the milk. Then add a drop of washing-up liquid in the centre of the bowl, and voilà, it's tie-dyed (but not drinkable!) milk.

176

sing the abc's

Sometimes it's good to let learning creep up on your little one. Sing the alphabet song as a knee-bouncing rhyme, a lullaby, a jazz song, or even a pop jingle. In two or three years when he's learning to read, he'll realize that he already knows the alphabet.

177

be a little teapot

Mix up the usual actions to this ditty by having one of you act as the teapot and the other as the tea cup.

I'm a little teapot,
Short and stout.
Here is my handle,
Here is my spout.
When I get all steamed up, then I shout,
"Tip me over and pour me out!"

178

tell it to the hand

Put on a glove puppet and use it to ask your child questions about her life and daily activities. She may share some novel insights with her funny new friend.

179

do a spot check

Try out this activity to get a better sense of how your toddler sees himself and his world. Without him knowing what you're doing, dab a dot of lipstick or face paint on his cheek or forehead, then put him in front of a mirror. Does he point at the spot on his image in the mirror or reach up to his own face? Sometime around the middle of your toddler's second year, he'll change from pointing to the spot in the mirror to raising his hand to touch his forehead. Once this happens, you know your little one has begun to develop a sense that he's "me", his own person, separate from everyone else.

180

18+

18 months & up

"give me a play date...
People my size are
fascinating. Encourage
me to share and to treat
my friends the way that
I like to be treated."

24+

from twenty-four months & up

Your two-year-old's personality is blossoming a bit more every day. Children this age know their own minds and aren't shy about sharing opinions and intentions with you. However, you are still the lens through which your child sees the universe; your ideas and ways of interacting with the world help to shape hers. The big task for your toddler at this time is to learn about herself – what she likes and how she can participate in the world more fully.

181

wash the dog

If your dog is well behaved and compliant, letting
your child help you wash her on a warm day can
be a riot — and everyone gets a bath at once! Have
on hand one dog, one toddler, the garden hose,
dog shampoo, lots and lots of towels, and oh,
yes — don't forget the camera.

182

march up and down

"The Grand Old Duke of York" is a great rhyme for older toddlers. You can bounce your child on your knee, let your fingers do the marching up and down his arms, or — even better for an upwardly mobile two-year-old — let him march up and down the nearest elevation, be it a cushion on the bedroom floor or a small hill in the park.

The grand old Duke of York,
He had ten thousand men.
He marched them up to the top of the hill,
And he marched them down again.

And when you are up, you are up,
And when you are down, you are down.
But when you are only half-way up,
You are neither up nor down.

183

work a wagon

While you're working in the garden, give your child a series of small pick-up and delivery jobs to accomplish with her wagon. For instance, you might say, "Pile up all the leaves you can in your wagon and take them over to the compost bin, please."

184

make a recording

When your child begins pretending to read – or babbling as he follows the words – he has reached a great milestone in pre-literacy. Don't stop reading to him, though. Instead, add spice to the activity by making a recording of yourself reading his favourite books so he can practise following along on his own when you're busy or away from home.

185

turn a negative into a positive

Your child's favourite word at this stage may be "no", a byproduct of her growing sense of self and desire to shape her world. Let her assert the power of "no" by asking absurd questions like "Are we standing in the ocean?" so she can respond with a resounding "No!"

186

kit out your child for fantasy

Add four or five pieces of fabric, in a range of textures and colours, to your child's toy chest. They should be the right size to make a bullfighter's cloak, a butterfly's wings, a picnic cloth, or a soft toy's blanket. You'll be amazed at all the dressing up and pretend-play uses he'll find for these simple bits of fabric.

187

feed the birds

Open a restaurant for the birds. Put up two or three bird feeders in your garden, making sure at least one of them is near your child's bedroom window. Let her help you keep the feeders filled with birdseed. Get a children's book about birds from the library and teach her the names of your most frequent visitors.

188

pamper your pets

It's not too early to involve your toddler in the care of family pets. A two-year-old can roll a ball or drag a piece of ribbon for the cat, or pour a cup of dried food into the dog's bowl. Children at this age also love to give treats, praise, and comfort to pets. Teach patience and gentleness, but keep your child safe by instructing him never to bother an animal that's eating or sleeping – and by supervising all close encounters of the furry kind. Don't over-react if a provoked cat scratches or a dog nips lightly – if you do, the child may become fearful. Say something like, "Ooh, Bob got scared when he felt his tail being pulled – let's pat him gently on the back next time and go and put something on that scratch."

189

shake some maracas

Help your child make maracas by dropping dried beans, lentils, or unpopped popcorn into a small plastic water bottle. Glue or tape the lid in place securely and watch as your child plays to make sure the lid doesn't come loose, as small items can be dangerous if they find their way into small mouths.

190

seek out shapes

Play a game to hone your child's ability to recognize shapes. Start with an easy one on a picture-book page ("Can you find something shaped like a circle?") and graduate to finding circles, squares, and other shapes out in the real world. "What about that flower box? That's right, it's a rectangle. What about the moon?"

191

try a freeze

Teach your child about the transforming power of cold by helping her pour fruit juice from a lightweight jug into small paper cups. Then freeze the juice, adding wooden lolly sticks once it's slushy. Waiting for these to freeze is hard, but worth it. It's also fun to let the cups harden outside on a very cold winter's day.

192

follow a pattern

Build on your child's growing understanding of patterns by getting ambitious with bead stringing. Using large wooden beads or cotton reels, suggest an easy pattern like green-blue-green-blue. Or ask him to put different colours in order – say, green-blue-green.

193

"crack me up...
I laugh when the people I
love laugh, and also if you
do something silly, like
offer a biscuit to my elbow."

194

solve a mystery

Hone your child's observation and logic skills by putting three soft toys in front of her and asking her to study them. Then ask her to close her eyes while you remove one. Say, "OK – you can look now – who's missing?" Once she masters the game, make it more challenging by adding more animals.

195

make things larger than life

Give your toddler a plastic magnifying glass so he can see things he's never seen before. Looking at his own hand, a teddy bear's fur, or blades of grass will open up whole new tiny worlds to him. A small unbreakable magnifying glass of his own might even become one of your child's prized possessions.

196

run a toy hospital

Two-year-olds are very caring and often want to mend things that are broken. Encourage your child's nurturing side by asking him to help you take care of soft toys or dolls. Let him tuck them into shoe-box beds while they recover, then get them all up to celebrate their restored health with a snack.

197

get handy

Coat your child's hands with non-toxic liquid paint
and ask her to press them onto a sheet of paper.
Handprints alone are great designs, but you can
help her be more ambitious by making tulips (fingers
pointing upward, with a brush-stroke green stem added
afterwards); butterflies (two hands, wrist to wrist, with
the fingers pointing away from each other); or
a sunflower (several yellow-painted handprints,
fingers spread out, with an added brown centre).

198

paint some rocks

Let your child paint smooth rocks with non-toxic paint.
He can decorate them with abstract designs or turn
them into creatures such as ladybirds, cats, or birds.

199

be a pea counter

This fingerplay sneaks in some counting practice:

Five fat peas in a pea pod pressed,
hold up one of your hands and make a fist

One grew, two grew, so did all the rest.
hold your thumb and fingers up, one by one

They grew and grew and did not stop
raise your hand in the air very slowly

Until one day the pod went POP!
clap your hands together loudly

200

make your child a star

Help build your toddler's sense of self by filming her
as she sings a song or tells a story. Play it back for
her so she can watch herself in action.

201

get bouncy

At around two years of age, your child may start being able to bounce a ball and catch it, or to catch one that you gently bounce to him. Just bouncing the ball is feat enough for a toddler, so don't be too worried about where it goes. And remember, larger, softer balls are usually easier for little hands to handle.

202

whip up a smoothie

Let your toddler help you make a fruit shake with a handful of fruit (bananas and berries are especially good), a scoop of ice cream or yogurt, and a splash of juice. Mix well in a blender, making sure that there are no lumps that could cause choking. A smoothie makes a great breakfast!

203

show off some art

Chances are that your little artist is producing a multitude of artworks at this stage. One idea to help you display his creative outpouring is to buy magnetic sheets at a craft shop and make fridge picture frames. Cut out concentric rectangles so that each becomes a slightly smaller frame – the tiniest one from the centre can set off a particularly nice detail. Or use his masterworks to decorate his room. You can also scan some of your favourite pieces into your computer and e-mail them to friends and family, display them as your monitor's "screensaver", or turn them into a digital slide show.

204

make designer shoelaces

Lay child-sized shoelaces on a paper towel and ask your child to help you add polka dots to them with non-toxic fabric paint (a pencil rubber makes a stamp of the right size). Once dry, thread them into her shoes.

205

be upwardly mobile

By now your child is probably getting pretty good at stair climbing, though going up is still easier than going down. He might still like to slide downstairs on his bottom, one step at a time, or walk down wedding-march style, so that both feet are on the same step at the same time. To build his confidence, practise going up and down together, but when you're not practising, keep the stairs in your home safely gated.

206

hop on a magic carpet

Cut the bottom out of a large paper bag, then cut along one folded edge to make a large rectangle. Cut a fringe into the two ends, then help your child colour designs on this "carpet" with non-toxic washable markers. Once he's on board his carpet, fire up his imagination by asking him what he sees below. "Are you flying over the house? Can you see the swings? Is that Tessie barking in the garden?"

24+

24 months & up

207

invent some rhymes

Start by letting your child finish familiar rhyming phrases, then add new ones. Once the concept is understood, take turns to add to a list of words that rhyme, such as cat, mat, bat, hat, and rat.

208

"teach me to play nice...
Show me the fun I can
have when I share my toys
and play with other kids."

209

sniff it out

The nose knows, so ask your child to close her eyes,
then stimulate her senses by asking her to sniff and
identify safe kitchen items. Vanilla, cinnamon,
and cocoa are good ones to try. Avoid peppers or
spicy things that might irritate her nose or eyes.

210

paint a biscuit canvas

Put a small amount of water in three bowls and
add drops of food colouring to each bowl to create
three different bright hues (the ratio of water to food
colouring should be about two to one). Let your
child use new, small paintbrushes to paint with
these colours on unbaked biscuits. Once they're
baked and cooled, let him eat his masterpieces.

POSTCARD

DEC 15
2006

211

make a postbox

Post may seem like magic to a toddler. Buy a small
toy postbox – or make one out of a shoe box – and
deliver notes or small toys to it from time to time.
Encourage friends and relatives to send postcards
to your child. Sort through your junk mail for
colourful envelopes to help fill her postbox.

212

have a drum session

Set up some percussion "instruments" outside or
in a playroom. Include anything you've got
that can be safely tapped, banged, or pounded:
cereal boxes, pots and pans, tin sand buckets,
blocks of wood, biscuit tins, washing-up
bowls, and empty plastic milk bottles are good
things to start with. Offer your little drummer boy
some spoons (wood, metal, or plastic) or
a wooden kitchen mallet, and belt out his
favourite tunes while he provides the percussion.
Or just sit back and enjoy his extended drum
solo. He's not just having fun, he's also improving
his sense of rhythm and eye-hand co-ordination.

24+

24 months & up

213

get picky

Place a dozen or so light objects – marshmallows, feathers, cereal – into a dish in front of your child. Give her a pair of blunt tweezers and show her how to pick up the objects and move them to another dish. This is a great way to sharpen fine motor skills, but since small objects are involved, watch closely.

214

sort things out

Lay out a dozen similar items, such as large beads or buttons, and ask your child to sort them by colour, shape, or size. Then ask him to sort by more subtle characteristics, like the number of holes in a button. Always be sure no small objects end up in his mouth.

215

plant a carrot top

Cut the tops from a few whole carrots (parsnip and radish tops work, too) about 2.5 cm (1 in) from the top. Help your toddler place them, cut side down, in a shallow dish. Pour in water until it's about halfway up the carrot tops. Continue to water and watch them every day. Soon feathery green leaves will reward your little gardener.

216

have a scavenger hunt

Give your child a magazine with lots of photos, then name a category — say, purple things, babies, food, or animals — and ask her to point out examples of those items as you look through the magazine with her.

217

draw out "hide and seek"

Don't be too quick to uncover the kid giggling behind the curtain or under the table. Instead, say aloud, "Wow, if only *[your child's name]* were here, he could tell me what a cow says." Keep the game going with different animals until he reveals himself – or is laughing so much it's impossible to pretend you don't know where he's hiding.

218

eat some ants

Cut celery sticks into short lengths and spread cream cheese or houmous into the hollow of each stick. Get your toddler to scatter raisin "ants" along the top of each piece. Who knew insects could be so tasty?

219

grow by leaps and...jumps?

Games and challenges that involve jumping are great for two-year-olds. They promote gross motor development, fine-tune their balance, and increase agility. They're also a great outlet for all that toddler energy. So draw a series of stars, polka dots, or flowers with pavement chalk, and see whether your child can jump from one to the next with both feet together. Later on, she might want to try hopping on one foot, then the other, or even try out the classic childhood game of hopscotch.

220

make instant puppets

Looking for a way to amuse your child in a hurry?
Use a non-toxic pen to draw faces on the pads of
his index fingers. He can pretend his two finger
people are talking to each other — and to you!

221

create sponge art

Cut new kitchen sponges into strips and circles.
Then let your child dip them into a puddle of
non-toxic liquid paint on a paper plate and press,
drag, or dab the sponges onto paper. A sponge
rolled into a tube and secured every 5 cm (2 in)
or so with elastic bands leaves an unusual
impression when rolled across paper. Try it out!

222

pack a picnic

Who cares if it's the same old cheese sandwich you were going to make for your toddler to eat at the kitchen table? And never mind that it's just in your garden. Pack your picnic nicely – basket, a checked tablecloth, and plastic cups. Outdoors, the juice is juicier, the cheese cheesier, the carrot sticks crunchier. Lie back with your child and search for sharks, trains, and alligators in the clouds, and you're well on your way to a memorable afternoon.

223

"give me a break...
If I'm worked up, take me away from the scene. Let me suck my thumb or clutch my blanket — or just hold me. Your touch is magic."

224

sing a song of sixpence

This short song has a lot packed into it — a cast
of royal characters and a flock of naughty blackbirds.

Sing a song of sixpence,
A pocket full of rye.
Four-and-twenty blackbirds baked in a pie.
When the pie was opened, the birds began to sing,
And wasn't that a dainty dish to set before a king?
The king was in his counting house,
counting out his money.
The queen was in the parlour,
eating bread and honey.
The maid was in the garden,
hanging out the clothes.
When along came a blackbird
and nipped her on the nose!
gently tap your little one's nose

24+

24 months & up

225

promote construction

The chances are your child is happy with ordinary stacking bricks, but this is a good age to introduce new building toys. Look for toddler versions of construction logs and connecting blocks, ones that are sized for small hands and fingers, and safe to mouth and bite. Don't expect the Taj Mahal to appear on the playroom floor just yet. For now, the appeal is making things connect, and having them stay together for a while — long enough to show off to an admiring parent.

226

dine in style

Even your little one will enjoy special dinners at home
from time to time, and it allows him to become familiar
with more formal settings. Put out a tablecloth, let
him help with an arrangement of flowers, play soft
jazz or classical music in the background, and
a meal of macaroni cheese becomes elegant.

227

explain change

Changes in your appearance can still be a little
startling for your two-year-old. A hat or a pair
of sunglasses might be fine, but if you were to
colour your hair or cut it very differently she might
need some reassurance that it's really you.
Explain the changes, and she'll soon adapt.

228

get the blues

Once in a while, devote a day to a specific colour.
If it's blue, for instance, dress in blue clothes, eat
blueberries, colour with blue crayons, and play with
blue toys. Look for blue things wherever you go and
make a game of pointing them out to each other.

229

make a portable banana split

Here's a snack that you can make together. Ask
your toddler to peel a banana, then give it to you
to cut in half crosswise. Help your child roll the
banana sections in melted chocolate (make sure it is
cool enough for little hands!) insert a wooden lolly stick
into each one for a handle, put them on greaseproof
paper, and freeze them for half an hour.

230

eat what you read

Prepare and eat a food inspired by one of your child's favourite books. You could serve up a Dr. Seuss special of green eggs and ham, or Maurice Sendak's *Chicken Soup with Rice*. Or why not taste a little of Goldilocks' beloved porridge?

231

wear a little nature

Kit out your toddler with flowers and weeds: make a daisy chain from daisies or a dandelion chain from dandelions, or a crown of wild grasses and flowers. If you live near sycamore trees, look for the seed "wings", which you can use to decorate your flower chains.

232

shape some sandwiches

Use a biscuit cutter or a knife to cut your child's sandwiches into interesting shapes. Or make a bi-coloured lunch by using one slice of white bread and one slice of wholemeal or granary.

233

set up a command centre

Write simple directions on slips of paper (for instance, "turn around", "hop like a bunny", and "bring me your toy cat"). Let your child pull the directions out of a plastic jar one at a time, and read them out to him. See how many directions he can remember and follow at a time. Let him select some commands for you, too.

234

put on a shadow play

Shine a bright light on the wall of a darkened room, and make shadow-puppet animals with your hands, using them to act out stories. Then help your child create some easy-to-make animal shadows of his own. Two good ones to start with are a rabbit (just tell him to hold up his fingers to show how old he is) and a butterfly (ask him to spread the fingers of both hands, holding them so that his thumbs are touching).

235

sing "wheels on the bus"

Where did this song come from? No one seems to know. But toddlers really love singing it.

The wheels on the bus go round and round,
Round and round,
Round and round.
The wheels on the bus go round and round,
All day long.

There are countless additional verses.
Here are some favourites:

The doors on the bus go open and shut...
The driver on the bus says, "Move on back"...
The wipers on the bus go swish, swish, swish...
The horn on the bus goes beep, beep, beep...
The baby on the bus cries, "Waa, waa, waa"...
The mummy on the bus says, "Shh, shh, shh"...

236

savour world cuisine

Get your child used to eating all kinds of cuisines early on. This will make it easier for your family to enjoy a variety of taste sensations while broadening her sensory experience. While a few toddlers happily cut their teeth on a spicy pizza, most little ones don't like strong tastes yet, so start with the milder dishes: Chinese noodles and sweet-and-sour chicken, gently spiced Indian biryani (rice) and nan (flat bread), or Middle Eastern houmous and falafel. Expand your child's cultural horizons by talking to him about the country the food comes from.

237

block out the pattern

Take eight toy bricks, four in each of two different colours. Lay out a pattern – perhaps two red blocks side by side. Give your toddler the remaining blocks and ask her to copy your model. Make a few more patterns for her to match.

238

sing to the moon

If you don't know the original tune to this traditional folk song, just improvise a melody.

I see the moon, and the moon sees me,
The moon sees somebody I'd like to see.
Bless the moon and bless me,
And bless somebody I'd like to see.

239

"treat my teddy with care...
Wash my favourite soft toy if
you must – but please do it
when I'm asleep, and put him
back into my bed before
I wake up in the morning."

240
watch and encourage

Let your child take his time to work out new things, such as solving a jigsaw puzzle. He's becoming more self-reliant — and loves to be encouraged when he succeeds. Step in only if he gets frustrated.

241
have fun with felt

Buy a felt board or make one by covering a large, sturdy piece of cardboard with felt from a fabric shop. Then buy some ready-made felt shapes, or cut out your own from pieces of felt: geometric shapes, animals, people, clouds, trees, aeroplanes, robots, dinosaurs, or whatever your child is interested in. This old-fashioned and low-tech way to design scenes and tell stories is perfect for amusing a two-year-old.

242

make more of the shore

Take your toddler to the beach and help her find her sea legs. Let her feel the surf around her ankles, and carry her securely into the water, gently reassuring her if she's nervous. Back on shore, search for treasures, then sort them: shells, driftwood, and smooth sea glass – even creatures like periwinkles might find themselves in her bucket. Help her gently examine the live things and return them to their original homes. If she finds rubbish, there's a lesson there, too – help her take it to the nearest rubbish bin.

24+

24 months & up

243

go out in the rain

Go outside every day, unless the weather's truly nasty. In fact, rainy walks can be the best kind. Put on boots and raincoats and linger over (and jump in) puddles, search for earthworms on the pavement, float leaves in little pools, and tip your heads back and catch raindrops on your tongues. Sometimes it's fun getting wet!

244

play "concentration"

Print out matching pictures from the Internet, lay them out face up (four pictures – two pairs – are enough to start with), then turn them face down and see if your child can turn over two that match. Add more pairs to keep the game challenging. Or try "Colour Concentration" with pairs of coloured cards, such as paint samples.

245

promote the chef

Let your toddler graduate to some real cooking duty. Supervise as he stirs muesli, mixes a salad, or uses a biscuit cutter to shape dough. Make his *sous-chef* status official by giving him a pint-sized apron of his very own.

246

sing about a bear

Explore new heights with this adventurous tune:

The bear went over the mountain,
sing three times in a row

To see what he could see.

He saw another mountain;
sing three times in a row

It was all that he could see!

247

visit a farmers' market

An outing to a market is as fun as it is educational.
Invite your toddler to help you find the things you
want: "Can you help me choose five apples?"
Buy something new to eat, and let her make some
choices of her own. Toddlers are more likely to
try things that they've had a hand in choosing.

248

run a car wash

Encourage your child's instinct to take care of his things by helping him gather his toy cars and trucks outside or in the bath for a clean-up. Give him a small bucket of soapy water and a sponge so he can wash them, then help him rinse them. For safety, stay with him and empty the bucket when he's finished.

249

mess it up!

Your toddler will love it when she hears you make a mistake. Saying "Oh, hey, great red shirt!" when she's wearing blue, or confusing song lyrics ("Sing a song of sixpence, a pocket full of sky...") will crack her up and promote her cognitive and language development.

250

get ambitious with bricks

Your child's ability to build with bricks gets a lot more sophisticated during this period. She now has the fine motor skills to build taller towers and longer trains. Show her architectural tricks, like how to add spaces to toy brick constructions by straddling a brick across two slightly separated ones underneath.

251

design a private cave

Drape a blanket over a card table so that it covers all four sides to the ground, then tuck up one side to make a doorway. Presto: a perfect cave for one (or one toddler, two soft toys, three trucks, and a biscuit). Throw in a blanket and a torch, and you've got deluxe toddler accommodation.

252

make eight-legged friends

Make an octopus doll out of an old clean sock.
Stuff the toe end with cotton-wool balls, then tie
a short bit of string or thread tightly under
the stuffed section so it holds its round shape.
Use scissors to cut fifteen slits from the top
of the sock to within 2.5 cm (1 in) or so of the
string. Add some eyes with a non-toxic marker.

253

play some water music

Fill six sturdy glasses with different amounts of
water, arranging them from least full to most full.
Show your child how to tap them gently with a metal
spoon to make music. Demonstrate how adding or
subtracting water changes the glasses' tones.

254

"help me be generous...
I'm starting to understand the joy
of giving — and I want to join in!
Teach me to share with other kids
or to make a present for a friend."

255

make a puzzling sandwich

Cut your child's sandwich into two or three irregular pieces. Challenge him to put the puzzle pieces back together – then he can eat the sandwich as a reward.

256

have a night out

When your toddler's up past dark, go out in the garden. Spread out a blanket (snuggle under another one if it's chilly), let your eyes adjust to the darkness, and talk about the moon and stars. Sing "Twinkle, Twinkle, Little Star" or "Fly Me to the Moon". Listen out for grasshoppers, frogs, and any night birds such as owls that live in your area.

257

make some playdough

Delight your child by making your own playdough.

3 cups flour
1½ cups salt
6 teaspoons cream of tartar
3 tablespoons vegetable oil
3 cups water
Few drops of food colouring in three colours

Combine all the ingredients except the food colouring in a large pot over medium heat. Stir constantly until the mixture pulls away from the sides of the pot and forms a ball. Remove from the heat and leave to cool. Turn the cooled dough onto greaseproof paper and knead it for a minute or so. Then divide it into three portions and knead in the food colourings to make each a different colour. The dough is now ready for your child to play with. Store each dough portion in separate bags in the fridge. Discard after a week or two.

258

load the animal train

Make a train by poking a small hole in each end of several shoe boxes and tying them together with thread or ribbon. Let your child be the conductor of the Animal Express and, with her whistle blowing, help her load up her toys for a ride.

259

share musical memories

Let your toddler hear the music of your own childhood. Dig out your old recordings or find some CDs of the songs you once listened to. You'll be astonished at how many of the songs you can still sing – and who knows, you may keep the musical tradition going for another generation.

260

bake a snake cake

Bake a cake in a Bundt pan (a tin with a raised centre, making a cake with a hole in the middle); when it's cool, cut it into three pieces. Have your child help you arrange them so the curves form a slithery snake, cover with green icing, and add cherry halves for eyes.

261

blow a harmonica

A harmonica is a great instrument for toddlers because it makes a noise whether they inhale or exhale. Blowing up and down the edge of the harmonica helps them learn about musical scales, too.

262

make bubbles

Pour bubble mix into a wide dish and demonstrate
how to blow bubbles with a bubble wand, or shape
your own from a pipe cleaner or toilet-paper tube
(these get soggy after a while, so have a few on
hand). Dip a plastic sieve in the soapy soup and
wave it to make dozens of tiny bubbles.

263

inspire a budding author

Your child may be starting to show an interest in
writing by pretending to write. Encourage her,
but don't worry about teaching the mechanics of
writing just yet. Give her crayons and paper, and
then ask her to read you what she's "written".

264

play "i spy" with your ears

Say, "I hear, with my little ear, two noises that are pretty near!" Ask your child to tell you two things she hears: a dog barking and a plane passing overhead, for instance. Make the game more challenging by asking for specifics, such as "I hear something that you ride in — what is it?"

265

try a coat trick

Putting on a coat can be hard for kids, so try this method: help your child lay his jacket, unbuttoned and face up, on the floor in front of him so that the collar opening is at his feet. Guide him as he bends over and inserts his arms into the sleeves, then help him flip the coat over his head so that it lands in the right position when he finishes putting his arms through the sleeves.

266

capture your child's day

Take photos of your child throughout the day, doing what he likes to do: playing, eating, going for walks, exploring the garden, picking up a sibling from school, helping out at home, and so on. Print or paste these pictures onto sheets of paper you can make into a booklet, or slide them into an album. It's guaranteed to become one of your toddler's very favourite books.

267

sing "london bridge"

Now's a good time to introduce simple musical rhymes and games that two or more people can play together. Two children (or adults) join hands to make the bridge under which the kids march as you sing. At "my fair lady", of course, one child is caught under the bridge and swayed gently during the chorus, then let go.

London Bridge is falling down,
Falling down, falling down.
London Bridge is falling down,
My fair lady.

[Chorus] *Take a key and lock her up,*
Lock her up, lock her up.
Take a key and lock her up,
My fair lady.

268

dine with a worm

At a restaurant, create a friendly "worm" dining
companion. Slip two straws out of their wrappers. Lay
the end of one wrapper over the end of the other so
they form an L shape, and fold the one on the bottom
over the one on top. Repeat, continuing to alternate
folds until both wrappers are completely folded up.
You'll have an accordion-like creature that can amuse
your little one with its antics. No wrapped straws?
Use paper strips from a sugar packet or a napkin.

24+

24 months & up

269

play a colour game

Expand your toddler's knowledge of colour by laying
out paper in bright crayon shades. Ask him to match
crayons to the papers as you both name the colours.

270

be a patron of the arts

For a two-year-old, drawing is more about the physical act than making a design that represents a flower or a person. Praise her for what she's doing and how much fun she's having doing it. Still, it's fine to interpret a little: "Wow, that looks like an apple to me — it's so beautiful!"

271

ride on a train

Line up the chairs in the dining room and invite your toddler — and any other family members who want to come along — to jump aboard the Chair Express, the fastest train in the house. Let him hand out paper "tickets" and collect them as riders get off and on.

272

set sail for animal island

The sofa is the boat, and the floor is Animal Island. If you disembark, you become an animal and must talk and move like a wild creature. Got something you want to say? Get back in the boat so you can communicate like a human being again.

30+

from thirty months & up

As your little one nears the end of his toddler months, he's becoming very much his own person, with his unique talents, gifts, and opinions. The speed at which toddlers pick up new skills and information can leave you breathless at times, and there's no slowing of the pace as he nears his third birthday. This is a golden age, with much of the willfulness of earlier toddler times making way for more relaxed interactions. You're still his favourite guide to his rapidly expanding world, so take time to enjoy this special stage together.

273

head down to the farm

Working farms that are open to visitors are worth searching out. Or perhaps you've noticed a place near you where animals graze in the fields. And a city farm with lambs and goats can seem quite exotic to city toddlers. Once you've found a suitable place, give your child a chance to see live versions of the animals in his storybooks. Wear boots, and always ask permission before attempting to touch or feed an animal. Wash your hands well afterward.

274

create fingerprint friends

Put out a pad of non-toxic washable ink (or non-toxic liquid paint on a paper plate) and ask your child to make fingerprints or thumbprints on paper. Once they're dry, use a marker to add details such as legs, tails, and petals to create people, animals, or flowers.

275

balance on a ball

Stimulate your child's sense of balance with a large vinyl "hopping" ball with a handle (sold at toy shops and sports shops). Although her feet may not yet touch the ground when she's on the ball, she can still sit and hold the handle. Bounce the ball gently with one hand, keeping her upright with the other.

276

use the power of nonsense

When your child is grumpy, challenge him to look you straight in the eye and very slowly say "cabbage, cabbage, cabbage" without laughing or cracking a smile. Almost impossible!

277

shake a rain stick

Scrunch a 1.5-m (5-ft) long piece of silver foil into the shape of a snake, then coil it into a spiral that fits inside an empty cardboard wrapping-paper tube. Securely seal one end of the tube with heavy paper and parcel tape. Pour ⅔ cup dried lentils into the open end, then securely seal that end, too. Stand the stick upright and listen to the "rain".

30+

30 months & up

278

"let's look at our feet...
It helps me develop
pride in my body if
you show me that
I am the same as you,
as well as unique."

279

build a fairy home

Go and look for fairy houses with your little one – are they under a twisted tree root, beneath the edge of the back step, inside a tangle of summer flowers? Bring the fairies a flat piece of bark for a table, moss for their beds, and acorn cups of water to drink. To help them improve their lodgings, use twigs, leaves, and other natural materials to build them a new home.

280

get heavy

"Heavy" work is great for developing your child's gross motor skills, and the accomplishment builds her self-esteem. So offer her a small pile of clothes to take to the wardrobe or a sturdy bag to carry her books from one room to another.

30+

30 months & up

281

cook some crazy crayons

Got lots of broken crayon bits? Line a fairy-cake tin with greaseproof paper. Peel the labels off the crayons and sort them into colours, putting each colour into a different cake cup. Fill the cups one-third full, then bake at 110°C (225°F), watching closely, until the bits have melted. Cool, peel off the paper, and then invite your child to use these crazy crayons.

282

play mad scientist

Spread newspapers on a table and give your little chemist bowls of water, spoons, empty plastic cups, and cups containing a little salt, sugar, flour, lemon juice, or water. Let her mix, concoct, stir, and taste, expanding her sensory knowledge of the world.

283

sing a song of shrubbery

Enjoy the classic version, then adapt this song to other acts, like, "This is the way we stroke the cat".

Here we go 'round the mulberry bush,
The mulberry bush, the mulberry bush.
Here we go 'round the mulberry bush
So early in the morning.

284

turn shopping into a game

To improve his matching skills, hand your child coupons and ask him to look out for the items shown while he's sitting in the shopping trolly. Offer hints like "I think you'll find that one in this aisle."

30+

30 months & up

285

admire the ducks

Make a trip to a duck pond to introduce your toddler to some feathered friends. See how many different kinds of ducks you can spot. If you sit quietly, they'll probably get used to you and your child. With luck, they'll come close so you can get a good look — and a good listen to their quacks. Invite her to imitate the ducks by doing a bit of quacking herself.

286

try out a different "i spy"

Play "I Spy" with a twist by focussing on what things do. For instance, you might say, "I spy something that plays music" (or that you can ride in, eat with, or sit on). It's a fun way to teach your child how things work.

287

put on a new face

Help your toddler place a medium-sized paper bag over his head, and gently use a crayon to mark where his eyes and mouth are. Take the bag off and cut openings at the marked spots. Give him crayons, non-toxic liquid paint, paper cut-out shapes, and glue so he can transform his new face into his wildest fancy, be it a tiger, a robot, or an alien.

30+

30 months & up

288

teach scissor savvy

Towards the end of their third year, some children may be able to cut paper with scissors. To encourage the development of that fine motor skill, make sure that the scissors are child-safe but not so dull that they result in a frustrating experience. Teach your child from the beginning that scissors are to be used only with an adult around and only while seated. Help your little artist by giving her tracing paper and holding the sides taut while she cuts a fringe on one edge. As her skill develops, cut out strips for her to cut into squares, and then help her glue them onto coloured paper to make a design.

289

sprout some initials

Help your child dampen a pad of cotton wool and put it in a dish. Sprinkle wheat seeds in the shape of his initials on the cotton wool. Help him keep them moist until they sprout and his initials come to life!

290

be penny-wise

Demonstrate some fun chemistry by dropping dirty pennies into a glass jar with a lid. Cover them with vinegar, then throw in a tablespoon of salt. Seal the jar and shake gently. Help your child shake the jar again once or twice later on, and those pennies will be clean by the next day. Remind her that no matter how shiny, pennies should never go in mouths.

30+

30 months & up

291

try out your spanish

Your child probably knows all the words to "Head, Shoulders, Knees, and Toes". Now try it in Spanish!

Cabeza, hombros, rodillas y pies
Rodillas y pies!
Cabeza, hombros, rodillas y pies
Rodillas y pies!
Ojos, orejas, boca y nariz.
Cabeza, hombros, rodillas y pies
Rodillas y pies!

292

teach about opposites

Ask your toddler to name the opposite of the word you say. Start with easy ones: girl, boy; on, off; big, small.

293

mix some colours

Put non-toxic liquid paint in the three primary
colours (red, blue, yellow) on a painter's palette
or around the edges of a plate. Demonstrate
how combining two colours creates a new one.

294

get boxed in

Phone a kitchen appliance shop and ask if a large
cardboard box can be saved for you – one that
originally contained an oven or a fridge. With a
knife (in your hands) and crayons (in your child's),
the box can become a supermarket, a puppet
theatre, a puppy's kennel, or a castle. With the right
props, his imagination can conjure up anything.

295

use your noggin

Kids love working out which item in a series doesn't fit with the rest. At this stage, you can help refine your child's logical thinking by making things harder. For instance, show her a trainer, a flip-flop, a sock, and a boot. The odd item might be the sock, because it's not a shoe. Or maybe it's the flip-flop, since you only wear it in the summer. The reasoning behind the answer may be as interesting as the answer itself.

296

make a paper bag doll

Loosely stuff a paper bag with newspaper. Seal this round "head" with tape, and attach a torso, arms, and legs cut out of paper. Ask your child to draw a face on her floppy new friend.

297

"respect my blankie...
When I want to comfort myself,
it reminds me of things that are
warm and snuggly (like you),
and helps me to keep going."

30+

30 months & up

298

collaborate on a book

Your toddler is full of stories, so team up on a book:
he dictates; you write; he illustrates. Put just a few
lines of text on each page, leaving plenty of room
for artwork. Once you finish the book, bind his
masterpiece in thick paper or card, then ask
him to add some cover art and choose a title.

299

make cleaning a game

When child's play turns into a major mess, enlist
your toddler in a cleanup — but make it fun. Ask her
to clean up all the red things, or all the square
things. Or play "take 10": put out a timer and see
how much she can tidy in 10 minutes, or ask her to
put away 10 items — and then perhaps 10 more.

300
play crayon-box bingo

On your next car journey, give your child a small box of crayons and use them to improve his colour sense. Ask him to watch the passing cars and, when he spots a red one, to hand you the red crayon, and so on. When the box is empty, he's won!

301
explore snackitecture

Serve up a plate of snacks that double as building supplies: cheese cut into cubes, peeled apple pieces, cut-up grapes, and bread sticks. See what sorts of structures your child makes out of these building materials before she gobbles them up.

30+

30 months & up

302

clap for miss mack

Enjoy this classic clapping rhyme any time. Face your toddler and mark the rhythm of the words "Mack, Mack, Mack" each time they're sung by clapping on your knees, or clapping your hands against your child's. Start slowly and see how fast you can get.

Miss Mary Mack, Mack, Mack,
All dressed in black, black, black,
Had silver buttons, buttons, buttons
All down her back, back, back.

She asked her mother, mother, mother
For fifty pence, pence, pence,
To see the elephant, elephant, elephant
Jump over the fence, fence, fence.

It jumped so high, high, high,
It reached the sky, sky, sky.
And it didn't come back, back, back
'Til the fourth of July, July, July!

303

make dandelion wishes

Teach your child how to make a wish
and blow the seeds off a ripe dandelion
head. Use a magnifying glass to study the
structure of the individual seeds. Then
pretend he's a dandelion: make a wish
out loud, blow on his hair, and encourage
your little seedling to spin around.

30+

30 months & up

304

assemble a car kit

Buy a metal pan with a plastic lid that slides on and off. Use the pan to store felt cut-outs of geometric shapes, people, animals, trees, clouds, and so on — all great for imaginative play. Add a drawing pad, crayons, and large magnetic letters (which can be used on the bottom of the pan). Adapt the kit to your child's interests by including her favourite diversions, be they dinosaurs, puppets, or books. When you're hitting the road, throw in a few healthy snacks such as carrot sticks and boxes of raisins.

305

whip up a parfait

Let your toddler make a healthy fruit sundae in a tall plastic parfait glass. Help her layer yogurt, sliced strawberries or other fruit, and something crunchy, like crumbled digestive biscuits. She'll enjoy making it almost as much as eating it.

306

lay the table

Help your child make paper cut-outs of a plate, knife, spoon, fork, and glass (you may need to do most of the cutting). Together, glue them into their proper places on a paper placemat. Take the paper place setting to a photocopy shop and get it laminated so your little helper can use it as a guide when he lays the table.

307

enjoy a concert

Toddlers love outdoor concerts, especially ones geared to kids. Bring a blanket or some folding chairs, a picnic, and a pillow and a soft toy in case the music is low-key. If it's lively, though, let her run around and dance as the spirit moves her, as long as she doesn't stray too far from home base — and your sight.

308

experiment with magnets

Magnets are wonderful toys for discovery play.
Go to the hardware shop and buy a variety of large
magnets. Don't be too quick to explain the principles
of magnetism to your child – he'll discover them
himself (and have more fun) by playing with them.
Do explain that because magnets are not kind to
watches, mobile phones, speakers, or computers,
they should be kept away from these items – and
that they never belong in his mouth!

309

make an impression

Potato prints are always a hit with kids. Cut a potato
in half, and cut out a shape. Put out non-toxic liquid
paint, and let your child make her mark.

310

"help me find myself...
It will be years before I
define my interests, so
it's great to try out lots
of new things now."

311

make edible initials

Buy an inexpensive set of letter-shaped biscuit
cutters, and use them to cut out your child's name
or initials from a piece of cheese on toast or
a sandwich. Yummy (and secretly educational)!

312

get creative with chalk

Keep some colourful pavement chalk in your car.
Most park and school groundskeepers are tolerant
about the use of chalk since the next rain will
wash the marks away, anyway. Draw lily pads, so
your little frog can hop from one to another. Make
square "pages", and tell a story in words or
pictures. Don't worry if the pavement's damp;
coloured chalks are at their most brilliant when wet.

30+

30 months & up

313

try some tongue twisters

See if your child can get his mouth around these:

Toy boat, toy boat, toy boat, toy boat.

Or:

She sells seashells by the seashore.

Or this one:

Three grey geese in the green grass grazing.

314

bake watermelon slices

Make crunchy slices of "watermelon" by using red food colouring to tint ready-made biscuit mix. Get your child to help you shape the mix into a roll and dip its edge in diluted green food colouring. Slice into semi-circles. Bake and munch away.

315

trace some leaves

Get your toddler to collect a handful of leaves from
your garden or the park. Then put out a few crayons
without their wrappers and some medium-weight
paper (plain photocopy paper works well). Lay the
leaves facedown (veiny side up) on the table and
put the paper on top of them. Help your child stroke
evenly over the leaf with the broad side of a crayon,
revealing the leaf's image on the paper. She might
like to try the same technique with other textured and
relatively flat items like tree bark, a fossil in a rock,
or the whorl of seeds in the centre of a sunflower.
Make a mobile by cutting out several of her favourite
rubbings, punching a hole in the top of each and
using thread to tie them along a chopstick or a dowel.

316

pick a peck

Check your local papers for "pick-your-own" farms. This is usually strawberries and raspberries, but some farms also offer vegetables. Fill your baskets together when you're in the fields, then pay and wash before you eat. Get on the farm's mailing list in your child's name: he'll be delighted to get a postcard telling him that the strawberries are ripe and ready for him to choose!

317

walk the plank

Lay a sturdy 5-by-15-cm (2-by-6-in) board or narrow table leaf that's about 90 cm (3 ft) long on two thick phone books, one under each end, so the board is roughly level and about 10 cm (4 in) off the ground. Guide your child as she practises walking across it. Once she's mastered that, give her sense of balance a real workout by trying it backwards!

318

get scientific in the bath

Scrunch a dry flannel or sponge into a large plastic cup. Help your child submerge the cup in the water, open end first, then bring it straight up again. Turn it over, and ask him to check the contents. Discuss how the sponge can be dry when it was under the water.

319

plant a box garden

You can use an actual window box, or just lie a milk carton on its side and cut off the uppermost side. Add some potting compost and help your child plant a few quick-to-grow seeds (pansies, marigolds, grass, and beans are all good choices). When the soil begins to feel dry, water it together. This is a good opportunity to start using a calendar, too – note the date on which you planted the seeds and help your child tick off the days until the first seedlings appear.

320

express puppy love

Singing about a new dog is almost as
much fun as having one.

How much is that doggie in the window,
The one with the waggly tail?
How much is that doggie in the window,
I do hope that doggie's for sale.

I don't want a fluffy little kitten;
I don't want a parrot that talks.
I don't want a bowl of little fishies;
You can't take a fish for a walk.

I just want that doggie in the window,
The one with the waggly tail.
How much is that doggie in the window?
I do hope that doggie's for sale!

321

grow a vine

Buy a sweet potato or a yam. (Bring home some extras to eat: baked for an hour at 200°C or, 400°F, yams make a healthy and naturally sweet toddler treat.) Holding the uncooked yam upright, stick in four toothpicks around the centre so that it will rest in the mouth of a jar with about half sticking out of the top. Add water to the jar until it's about halfway up the yam, and put the jar in a sunny spot. Ask your child to help you top off the water level if it gets too low. It may take a week or two for the yam to sprout, but once it does, it will grow rapidly. Soon you'll have a lush vine — and your child will have a better appreciation of nature's magic.

322

play a xylophone

Buy a small xylophone, the type with metal keys that are often used in primary schools. It will last forever, and your child will have a great time just playing with it. And she'll sharpen her eye-hand co-ordination and develop her musical ear while she's at it!

323

teach about time

Old-fashioned analogue clocks, especially those with sweeping second hands, often fascinate toddlers. Talk about how the face of the clock is a circle, point out the big and little hands, and count out the numbers, reminding him that the little hand should be on the "7" before he gets out of bed in the morning.

324

test the tastebuds

Try this sensory-exploration game when you're in the kitchen. Have your little one close her eyes tightly and open her mouth. Pop something yummy in, then see if she can guess what it is. A piece of banana? A chocolate chip? Now ask her to hold her nose and try again — what differences does she notice?

325

draw some finger actors

Create instant puppets by cutting the fingers off a white cotton glove and putting them on your child's fingers. Use non-toxic cloth markers to draw faces and other features on them to help bring the puppets to life. Make a whole cast of characters, then let your toddler make up his own drama.

326

"be my home base...
I'm trying out my independence,
and may wander away, but I'll
usually come back on my own.
Keep an eye on me, though."

30+

30 months & up

327

make art central

Stock a small chest of drawers or a bookcase with open-topped boxes full of child-friendly art materials, and your toddler will always have the tools to express her creative side. Include copy paper, newspaper, construction paper, scraps of wrapping paper, and sheets of cardboard. Add boxes of "found" objects such as ribbon, thread, extra large buttons, and lolly sticks for making collages and other craft projects. Keep an "Ask First!" box of art supplies like non-toxic liquid paints, markers, and crayons — a repository for items she can use only with an adult's supervision — nearby but safely out of reach.

328

guess what's in the basket

Even an older toddler may not be ready for something as abstract as "20 Questions", but if you put a familiar object in a basket and cover it with a cloth, she might be able to guess what it is with a few hints. Then let her put something in the basket and challenge you to guess the mystery item's identity.

329

make a "bunny" salad

Show your child that making food can be fun. Ask him to put a clean lettuce leaf on a plate, then top it with a peeled pear half, cut side down. Give him two thin slices of carrot to stick into the pear's narrow end to make bunny ears. Add raisin eyes, a sliver of cherry or strawberry for a nose, and a dollop of yogurt for a tail.

330

take in a movie

Sitting through a "real" film in a big, dark cinema
might be too demanding for a toddler. Instead,
look for showings of short children's films
at a local community centre. Or have family film
night at home with a DVD or a video.

331

get artsy

Collect the raw materials for a sculpture: wooden
spools, empty milk cartons, and clean lolly sticks, for
example. Then let your budding artist loose with non-
toxic craft glue. The chances are your child will be more
of an abstract expressionist than a realist, but at this
age, most of the joy (and fine motor skill development)
comes from just manipulating the shapes.

332

enjoy a jumpy rhyme

By now, your child might be too old for knee-bouncing rhymes. Then again, she might not!

Five little monkeys jumping on the bed.
One rolled off and bumped his head.
Mama called the doctor and the doctor said,
[Sternly] *"No more monkeys jumping on the bed!"*

for subsequent verses, count down until
you reach "one little monkey"

One little monkey jumping on the bed.
She rolled off and bumped her head.
Mama called the doctor and the doctor said,
"No more monkeys jumping on the bed!"

333

play pizza parlour

Kids love doing things that reflect the grown-up world,
so let your child try his hand as a pizza chef. Cut the
"ingredients" for a pizza from felt: light brown dough,
maroon pepperoni, grey mushrooms, green peppers,
and white cheese. Complete the effect with a few pizza
boxes bought at your local real-life pizza take-away.
Give him an apron so your little chef can serve his
creation in style. *Buon appetito!*

334

make instant friends

Introducing...the foolproof origami puppy! Fold a square of paper in half, corner to corner, so it makes a triangle. With the folded edge of the paper facing away from you on the table, fold down the two outer corners so they look like floppy ears. Use a crayon or a pen to add eyes and a nose, and you've made a new chum for your child. Make a whole litter of puppies, which your child can decorate with spots or stripes.

335

study the world of ants

Sprinkle sugar on the ground near an anthill, then give your child a plastic magnifying glass and let him spy on the ants as they gather their treasure. Do the ants have different jobs? Are they a good team?

336

start a collection

Help your child explore her interests through collecting. A beach trip might spark a shell collection, a trip to the park a rock collection. Or maybe she always brings back the same type of souvenir from family holidays: a T-shirt or a snow shaker. Whatever she collects, help her display her keepsakes, perhaps in clear plastic jars or boxes on an open shelf.

337

string some snacks

Let your toddler make an edible necklace by threading O-shaped cereal pieces and other stringable treats on twine or kitchen string.

338

belt out a funny tune

Older toddlers relish the sophisticated wordplay of this venerable kids' song.

I knew a man called Michael Finnegan;
He had whiskers on his chinnegan.
They fell out and then grew in again,
Poor old Michael Finnegan.
Begin again!

339

make a personal puzzle

Glue one of your child's drawings onto cardboard and cut it into a variety of shapes for him to fit together. Or buy a blank jigsaw puzzle and get him to draw on it, take it apart, and reassemble it.

30+

30 months

340

"money's a bit of a mystery... But it's not too soon to get me started on saving. Help me count my coins – and maybe buy a treat with them!"

341

map it

Teaching basic map skills stretches your child's cognitive skills and spatial awareness, and it will help her get her bearings in your neighbourhood. Grab a drawing pad and take a walk with your toddler on your street. Take a bird's-eye view: "If we were flying, what would we see next to our house when we looked down from the sky? Yes, we'd see your friend Susan's house. What else would we see?" Sketch the street and draw boxes labelled "My House", "Susan's House", and "Playground", for example. When you get home, cut out simple paper versions of these landmarks and see whether your child can help you place them in the right order. "Remember what came next? Was it the library or the hardware shop?"

342

construct a riding route

If your toddler is ready to ride a tricycle, help him gain skill on his new wheels by using pavement chalk to chart a course for him to follow in an unoccupied paved area. Include turns and stop signs. He'll relish the challenge – and his newfound mobility.

343

team up to make dinner

Divide homemade or shop-bought pizza dough into fist-size balls and pat them thin and round. Put out bowls of tomato sauce, grated cheese, olives, salami slices – whatever your family prefers on a pizza. Ask your toddler to take the family's orders for personal pizzas and let her arrange the desired toppings. You can take it from there.

344

look underwater

Make a viewing scope so your young marine biologist
can study the shallow water at the beach or a pond.
Cut both ends off a milk carton, cover one end with
tautly stretched cling film, and tape the edges to the
sides of the carton with waterproof tape. Hold your
child while he submerges the cling-film–covered end in
the water and peeks through the other end. Hello, fish!

345

be an answer person

This age ushers in an explosion of endless
questions. Answer them as patiently as possible
since they're the way your child is expanding
his vocabulary and learning about the world.

346

root for the home team

On a clear day, stroll with your child to a nearby playing field and take in a sporting event — any local football, cricket, or baseball game will do. She'll thrive off of the spectators' bustling energy and enjoy clapping and singing along with the team chants. Be sure to apply generous amounts of sunscreen and to find a seat that's not in the path of stray balls.

347

tie-dye socks

Put a half-dozen pennies or marbles in one of your child's white cotton athletic socks, then do the same with its mate. Gather the fabric around each object to form a lump and tie each lump with string or an elastic band. Mix fabric dye in a bucket (disposable paper buckets are available in some hardware shops), and let your child drop them in. Submerge the socks, following the directions on the dye packet. Rinse the socks well, then dry them in a warm dryer. Untie the strings, and the tie-dyed socks are now ready for your child to model – and they're guaranteed to please even the most style-conscious toddler.

30+

30 months & up

348

gather a dressing-up kit

Kids love dressing up, and they don't need much encouragement to imagine themselves as bus drivers, animals, or magicians. Gather up old Halloween costumes, out-of-date dresses, jackets, even wallets complete with business cards, and whatever other clothes and accessories you can donate to the cause. You'll be surprised at how much magic there is in your old winter hat!

349

whip up oobleck

Are you and your toddler ready for some messy
science? Set yourself up – either outdoors or on
a newspaper-covered kitchen table – with a wide
plastic container, two boxes of cornflour, a jug of
water you've tinted with food colouring, and a
wooden spoon. Pour the cornflour into the container,
and slowly stir in just enough water to make a
mixture that's roughly the texture of dough. You've
just made Oobleck! Now let your child roll up her
sleeves and play with it (you can join in, too). Gather
up a handful and squeeze it into a hard ball, then
open your hand and watch it dribble back into ooze.

*Note: don't pour Oobleck down the drain! When
you're finished, dispose of it by pouring it into an old
milk carton and discarding it with the rubbish.*

350

shine some starlight

Find an illustration of a simple constellation, such as Orion or the Big Dipper, in an astronomy book or online. Use a skewer or a small nail to poke holes in the bottom of a paper cup to correspond to the constellation's shape. At bedtime, darken your child's room and let him shine a torch through the holes in the cup to project "stars" onto the ceiling.

351

create egg box creatures

To make an insect menagerie, cut a cardboard egg box into pieces that have different numbers of cup-shaped sections. Punch some holes in strategic places, then invite your child to fashion brightly coloured pipe cleaners into legs, antennae, and wings. A one-cup section might become a ladybird; a three-cup piece makes a great caterpillar.

352

play car park

Arrange pieces of coloured paper "parking spaces" in a line and help your child "drive" toy cars onto them. Ask her to park each car on the coloured square that matches it. Then mix up your instructions: "Please park the yellow truck in the red parking place."

30+

30 months & up

353

visit the playground

Playgrounds have far more equipment for
climbing, swinging, and exploring than you're
likely to have in your own garden. So visit a
few playgrounds geared to the needs of smaller
children. After trying them out, give your child a
choice: "Would you rather go to the playground
with the pretend castle or the one with the giant
turtle in the sandpit?" Don't forget to take snacks
and drinks along on your adventure.

354

" **play with numbers...**
In a shop or on the
street, stop for a moment
and say, 'I spy something
with a number 3.' Then
praise me when I find it! **"**

355

shake a bit of butter

This is a good family or group activity, since the shaking can take a long time and goes much faster if you take turns. Fill a plastic jar that has a tight-fitting lid with very cold double cream until it's two-thirds full. Drop in two or three clean glass marbles to help mix the cream, then start shaking the jar briskly. You can recite this rhyme to help pass the time:

Come, butter, come,
Come, butter, come.
Baby's standing at the gate,
Waiting for a butter cake.
Come, butter, come!

Keep taking turns, taking over from your toddler when he gets tired or bored. In 10 to 15 minutes, the cream will turn to butter. Strain out any remaining liquid, and use a wooden spoon to mix in salt to taste. Try your homemade butter on toast or crackers.

356

read to the dog

Budding readers may not know all the words in a
familiar picture book, but the dog doesn't know that.
So sit her down with Fido and let her "read" to him.
This activity works with cats or toy animals, too!

357

decorate snazzy cupcakes

Bake some cupcakes, then ask your toddler to help you try out these fun decorating ideas:

Add red food colouring to white icing and use it to make the cupcakes look like apples.

Tint the icing blue, ice the cupcake, then sprinkle half of it with crushed wafer crumbs: sea and sand, just like the beach!

Turn a white-iced cupcake into a football by painting on stitches with black icing.

358

make a puppet theatre

Hem 90 cm (3 ft) or so of fabric by folding the
top 5 cm (2 in) down and stitching it in place.
Thread a tensioned curtain rod through the hem,
and position the rod horizontally in a doorway,
about 90 cm (3 ft) or so from the floor. Provide lots of
different kinds of puppets and props to make it
fun and interesting. Voilà – instant puppet theatre!

359

get your potatoes out

For toddlers' group games, demonstrate the
time-honoured method of determining who goes
first. Make all the children present extend their
fisted "potatoes", and count around using the song
"One Potato, Two Potato..." to decide who is first.

30+

30 m

360

coach your toddler

New challenges might sometimes leave your toddler feeling a bit frustrated. Try these four steps to help him master a new task, be it zipping up his coat, pouring milk, or putting on socks:

1. Get his attention, then demonstrate and explain the task in simple language.

2. Give him materials that make the task easier — perhaps a big zip pull, or a small jug into which you can pour the milk before he tries to pour it into his glass.

3. Break the task into steps to make it easier: "Look, scrunch up the top of the sock first, like this."

4. Give him encouraging feedback: "You did that part just right — now pull the zip up a little higher, and you've got it!"

361

make some tiny friends

If you greet insects with happy surprise
and curiosity, your child will do the same. Watch
butterflies in the garden together, and let caterpillars
walk on your hands. Show caution, not fear, around
potentially stinging insects like bees, and your
child will learn not to panic at the sight of them.

362

ride through the car wash

After your child has watched the family car go through
the car wash a few times, see whether he'd like to ride
inside the car with you as it goes through its soapy
shower. Don't push it if he finds the idea a bit scary,
but if he'd like to try it, explain that it will be a little
noisy, and narrate everything that's happening.

363

try out some humour

Jolly your child out of a bad mood by breaking into song – this classic usually does the trick.

Nobody likes me, everybody hates me,
I'm going to the garden to eat worms!
Nobody likes me, everybody hates me,
Going to the garden to eat worms!
Big fat slimy ones, little bitty skinny ones,
I'm going to the garden to eat worms!

364

design yourself

Take pavement chalks to a playground. Get your child to lie on his back, and trace his outline. Then give him the chalks so he can "dress" the figure and add realistic or fantastic facial features.

365

hang out at a café

Even your toddler likes to go where
somebody knows her name — and
what she'd like for breakfast. So make
a regular café date with your little
one, perhaps every Saturday morning.
Let her order something she doesn't
normally eat at home. Chat with the
staff, linger over milk and coffee, and
leave a nice tip so they'll be happy to
see the two of you again next week!

30+

30 months & up

index

a, b, c

d, e, f

g, h, i

j, k, l

about gymboree

Since 1976, Gymboree has helped parents and children discover the many pleasures and benefits of play. Based on established principles of early childhood education and administered by trained teachers, Gymboree Play & Music classes emphasize the wonder of play in a non-competitive, nurturing environment. Gymboree, which runs its interactive parent-child programmes in more than 27 countries, has contributed to the international awareness of the importance of play.

consulting editors

Dr. Roni Cohen Leiderman is a developmental psychologist specializing in emotional development, positive discipline, and play. For more than 25 years, she has worked with children, families, and professionals. She is associate dean of the Mailman Segal Institute for Early Childhood Studies at Nova Southeastern University in Fort Lauderdale, Florida, USA, and the mother of two children.

Dr. Wendy Masi is a developmental psychologist specializing in early childhood. She has designed and implemented programmes for nurseries, families with young children, and early childhood professionals for more than 25 years. The mother of four children, Dr. Masi is dean of the Mailman Segal Institute for Early Childhood Studies at Nova Southeastern University.

author

Nancy Wilson Hall, the mother of two children, is the award-winning author of eight books about babies, children, and families.

illustrator

Christine Coirault, a children's book illustrator based in London, is the illustrator of *How Do I Say That?* and the author of *The Little Book of Good Manners*.

photographer

Tosca Radigonda has made a career of capturing the beauty, warmth, and grace of children and families. She lives in Austin, Texas, with her husband and their son.